Bitten by the Bullet

Bitten by the Bullet

cx Motorcycle Adventures in India cx

Steve Krzystyniak and Karen Goa

NEW HOLLAND

Contact details

Indian Motorcycle Adventures Ltd.
40 O'Brien Road, Rocky Bay, Waiheke Island
New Zealand Tel: 64 (0) 9 372 7550
E-mail: gumby@ihug.co.nz
http://homepages.ihug.co.nz/~gumby

First published in 2002 by New Holland Publishers (NZ) Ltd
Auckland • Sydney • London • Cape Town

218 Lake Road, Northcote, Auckland, New Zealand
14 Aquatic Drive, Frenchs Forest, NSW 2086, Australia
86–88 Edgware Road, London W2 2EA, United Kingdom
80 McKenzie Street, Cape Town 8001, South Africa

www.newhollandpublishers.com

ISBN: 1 877246 75 1

Publishing manager: Renée Lang
Project editor: Amy Palmer
Editor: Mike Wagg
Cover design: Craig Kinney
Cover illustration: Soni Gopal
Design and typesetting: Graeme Leather

1 3 5 7 9 10 8 6 4 2

Printed by McPherson's Printing Group, Australia

Travel and motorbikes are in Steve Krzystyniak's blood. He is now based on Waiheke Island in New Zealand. Together with his wife, Lily, he makes a living operating adventure motorcycle tours in Asia.

Karen Goa is an Auckland-based travel and fiction writer. Born in Saskatoon, Canada, Karen continues to travel both northern and southern hemispheres, usually on more than two wheels.

For Sally

Acknowledgements

My heartfelt thanks go out to Peter and Dawn Green for making the connection, to my wife Lily for her saintly patience and to Karen for all her support and guidance. Lalli Singh, without your friendship, understanding and tolerance, the Indian part of our lives would never have grown so – namaskar.

– Steve Krzystyniak

I'm very grateful to Steve for his prodigious raconteuring and good humour, and also to the Indian people we met and our fellow bikers for sharing their stories. Special thanks go to my husband Ken (despite the ditch episode) for his love, encouragement and motorcycling enthusiasm.

– Karen Goa

We are also indebted to the following people who provided such excellent photographs: Owen Haskell, Jenny Cooper, David Hunter, Wynne Norgrove, Ravi Chauhan, and Ken Goa.

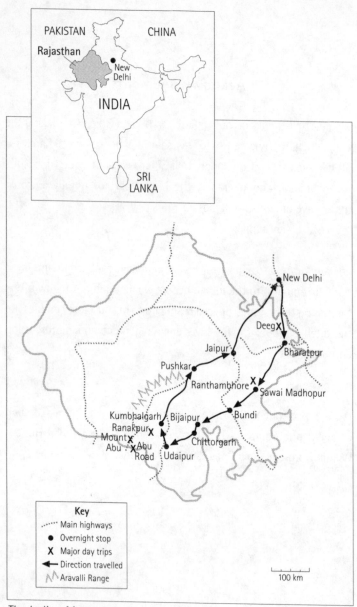

The Indian Motorcycle Adventurers' route across Rajasthan.

Chapter One

'Welcome to India!'

I shook the hands of the weary group emerging into the crowded New Delhi Airport arrivals hall carrying their crash helmets.

'Just gather together over there and we'll head outside in a minute. Keep all your baggage close to hand,' I shouted, pointing over the crowd to one of the few more or less clear pieces of real estate in the hall. They pushed tentatively through the massed ranks of hotel drivers and families awaiting their loved ones, who were completely blocking the exit despite the pointless efforts of a couple of tired looking security guards to keep the exit clear. A couple of the group looked distinctly dubious about the prospect of venturing into the dark car park beyond the hall windows.

'Any problems Lil?' I asked my partner, who'd just appeared through the gate. Lily, a registered nurse and an experienced tour leader, had shepherded the group from Auckland to Bangkok for a day, then on to India. I'd already spent several days in New Delhi getting bikes prepared and confirming our travel and accommodation arrangements for this trip, our seventh *Indian Motorcycle Adventures* tour to Rajasthan.

'So far so good. They've all had a great time in Bangkok. No one's been sick, missed a flight or got too lost,' reported Lily. 'They're a pretty good group.'

Over the next three weeks Lily and I would be responsible for safely guiding this group of Westerners, mainly New Zealanders, riding Enfield Bullet motorcycles along the back roads of the vast Indian state of Rajasthan. Our itinerary would take us to the very heart of this ancient land of the maharajas, where warrior Rajput princes once rode armoured elephants into battle across sun-scorched plains. We'd be taking our tour across this same terrain, but on the 1950s-style Bullets.

I counted heads, a tour leader's obsession, and getting the correct number, called out 'Has everyone got their bags and helmets? Right then, let's go.'

We stepped out into the hazy midnight air and manoeuvred ourselves and our baggage through the crush of Indians clustered in the car park. There were more than a few coughs and splutters from the group as they breathed in their first lungfuls of New Delhi's exhaust-laden air.

'You want taxi, hotel room, rickshaw, money change?' came the refrain of desperate touts from all sides, some of them even trying to grab our bags and whisk them off to their taxis. Ignoring these offers we led the way to the car park where Ratan, our driver, was waiting.

If the New Delhi airport flustered new arrivals during their first moments in India, then riding along in the New Delhi traffic would be suicidal, even for experienced motorcycle riders. Lily and I thought it best to ease our clients in gently to both India and the traffic, so we'd arranged for Ratan to pick up everyone in the Sumo backup vehicle and take us to our hotel in New Delhi on the first night. That would be enough excitement for one evening. Our first motorcycle ride would come the day after tomorrow in the quiet town of Bharatpur, two hundred kilometres south of New Delhi.

We arrived at our van to discover it completely boxed in by other cars, with less than an inch to spare front and rear. Their drivers were nowhere in sight.

'How do we get out of *this*?'

'If everyone can just get into the van, Ratan will sort it out.'

Ratan, a New Delhi-ite, knew all the tricks. With a little help from one or two of the more eager clients, he pushed the offending cars back and forth until there was a gap large enough to squeeze our van through.

'It's good luck those cars were left in neutral,' was the general comment.

'That's not luck, that's the usual system,' I said. Leaving the cars in neutral so that other drivers could push them around nearly doubled the parking capacity of the car park. It was a typical Indian solution to a typical Indian problem.

By now it was well past midnight and visibility was poor. In his usual imperturbable style Ratan drove fearlessly into the thick of it. Our clients were about to have their first taste of Indian traffic.

Even at this time of night, brightly painted Indian-made Tata trucks laden to overflowing with all manner of cargo still rumbled through the dark streets. They zoomed along at what seemed like wildly imprudent speeds for such overloaded vehicles. 'Blow horn please' read the signs painted on the tailgates of many of these trucks. A few clients raised their eyebrows.

'These trucks don't have mirrors,' I explained. 'If you want them to know you're there, you have to blow your horn. If you don't, you may get run down.'

At that moment two large trucks, multi-tone horns honking, swung out from behind us at the same time, each racing side by side to pass us. Ratan edged over as far as he could without crashing into any power poles alongside the road. The two trucks roared past, one diving back into the lane in front of us while the other jousted with an oncoming bus.

'Jesus!' 'Did you see that!' 'What a pack of nutters!'

'What d'you think?' I asked. 'Can you handle riding in this?'

There was a long, uneasy silence.

❀

The clients who came on our tours fell into two broad categories. Most were keen motorcycle enthusiasts who loved to ride, and if the ride took them somewhere unusual or interesting, so much the better. Often these bikies had never visited semi-developed countries before. The other type tended to be travellers first and motorcycle riders second. These clients wanted to see India semi-independently, without the limitations of an organised bus tour or the frustrations of public transport. Men inevitably outnumbered women, although a few women either came along as pillions or, more rarely, rode their own motorbikes.

The average age of our tour groups was usually in the high fifties. This was a surprise to many people, including ourselves, who thought of motorcycle riding as a young man's sport. In reality, many of our clients had ridden motorcycles all their lives. Some had been riders decades ago and had rekindled their interest in motorcycles once their children had grown up or they'd freed up some retirement time and money. What they might have lacked in youth, these riders made up for in experience and enthusiasm.

But even the most skilled riders didn't seem eager to leap out of the van onto a bike on their first night in New Delhi.

'If you're not keen on a bike right now, maybe you could try an elephant, like the maharajas,' I suggested, pointing to the side of the road where a couple of large shapes loomed in the faint orange glow of the streetlights. The odd flash of red light caught my eye as they moved around.

The sight of elephants on the streets of New Delhi caused a near riot inside the van.

Ratan stopped just ahead of the beasts, and we all scrambled out. Two elephants with the howdahs on their backs piled high with vegetation stood patiently by the side of the road next to the airport boundary fence. As we walked closer we could see that the elephants wore battery-powered red bicycle lamps strapped onto their rear right feet – the 'flashes' of light we'd seen. The elephants leisurely helped themselves to the long grass and other greenery growing along the roadside. On the other side of the fence, we could faintly glimpse their mahouts cutting long swathes of grass and other plants with machetes.

'There aren't too many places to get free elephant feed in New Delhi, so they come down to the airport at night to cut the grass around the airport perimeter,' I explained.

'Isn't it a bit of a security hazard having elephants and their riders all over the airport?' someone asked. 'There's nothing to stop them wandering onto the runways.'

'I think it's more a question of the airport turning a blind eye and saving costs on the mowing around the edges,' I replied. 'You'll find that people over here use their common sense and don't need signs to tell them not to walk on runways.'

The group was still buzzing with elephant talk when we finally turned into a narrow street and pulled up outside our hotel. The street was bright with the lights strung up for Diwali, the just-finished 'Festival of Lights', celebrated with masses of sparklers and the lighting of earthenware lamps to welcome Lakshmi, the goddess of wealth. Even at this late hour the street looked mysterious and exotic. It seemed like hours before we could finally settle everyone in their rooms and fall into bed ourselves.

The next morning, I awoke early and climbed to the rooftop restaurant to wait for the first of our exhausted clients to straggle up for breakfast. Even in the New Delhi treetops the 'traffic' was full on. Brown hawks courted each other in the tops of the tall trees, while tiny squirrels scampered back and forth between the branches, keeping a sharp eye on the hawks. Down below, a thin man performed ablutions in the bare dust of a courtyard, and a lone motorcyclist buzzed down the street. A curved piece of perspex was strapped onto his face with a bungy cord, and his turban perched on top – an Indian version of a helmet. On the other side of the street, on the pavement, a group of men chopped vegetables into pots to be cooked and sold as lunches later that morning.

Once everyone had emerged onto the rooftop, a breakfast of parathas, vegetable sabzi, or curry and yoghurt was served to us by languid waiters. Finally replete, we urged everyone to pack and start loading the Sumo that had just arrived to take us out of Delhi to Bharatpur.

Down on the street, our group attracted a great deal of attention from street urchins and shoeshine-wallahs who all gathered around pressing for 'one rupee, one pen', or 'shoes polish' as we struggled to squeeze our bags through the throng and onto the vehicle. I rushed around ensuring that the bags were all secure and that everyone had cleared everything out of their rooms and that bills had been paid and porters tipped.

I paused for a moment to take in the bustling early morning scene of frantic preparations that had become almost commonplace to me. Looking at Alex, a sprightly sixty-something wharfie, I raised my eyebrows in mock exasperation.

'How did you end up doing this as a job, Steve?' he asked, waving his hand at the chaos.

It was a question I sometimes still asked myself.

∞

My fascination with motorcycles began at an early age, in England. At thirteen, a friend and I dragged a rusty and incomplete Villiers 175cc motorbike from the waste ground near the Grand Union Canal in Southall. Although we eventually managed to start the engine, lack of funds prevented the project from proceeding further.

My first real rides were around west London, lacking both helmet and driving licence, on a tiny Honda 50 owned by Fred, my brother-in-law to be. Fred, who lived in Stratford in east London, was so enamoured of my sister Anita that every Friday evening he'd ride his little machine across the city to spend the weekend with her. I'd often contrive to casually drop in on them, unannounced and unwelcome. At this stage in their romance Fred's resistance to my not-so-subtle hints to ride his bike, leaving Anita and him alone, was extremely low. Usually within half an hour of playing gooseberry I'd be unleashed upon the travelling public of west London, a boy racer, crouched low over the handlebars of this underpowered moped.

For many months I dodged the not-so-long arm of the law on this machine, desperately trying to impress the students from the nearby girls' school with my 'hog'. It all came to an abrupt halt one summer's evening with an encounter with a couple of panda cars and an official caution to both Fred and myself at Greenford Police Station.

Next came a 1949 rigid-framed Triumph 500, along with my first job as an apprentice in a mechanical workshop and a loan of twenty pounds from my employer. Regrettably this loan was only ever half repaid, the job losing its glamour after the first three months or so. This bike had had the steering head raked back and extended front forks attached in the American 'easy rider' style. To me it looked incredibly cool, but it had the unfortunate attribute of being almost totally unrideable except in a straight line. This was fine for the highways of America but disastrous on the busy streets of west London. It quickly became a worthless and broken wreck after several minor but crunching accidents.

Bailing out of London a few years later, I spent much of my teens and early twenties on the Spanish island of Mallorca in the Mediterranean. Along the way I acquired a Spanish-built Ducati single-cylinder 175cc. This was a truly marvellous machine, reliable and plenty fast enough for the twisting roads in the north of the island where I lived amongst an eclectic expat community of artists, musicians and drug-takers. A near-lethal combination of the latter activity, ludicrously cheap alcohol and young testosterone put paid to that bike, almost taking me with it.

Soon after, I managed to get the money together to take my long-planned 'trip of enlightenment' to India, as so many other

Westerners were doing at the time. India was a revelation, to say the least. After a few days in Bombay, strolling bug-eyed around the bazaars of that manic city, I boarded the creaky and smelly old ferry down to Goa, then the hippie capital of the world. Here, I found a frenzied hyperactive scene of pseudo gurus, shamans, drug-dealers and beach parties. I threw myself into this with relish.

Ever on the lookout for interesting motorcycles I soon spied the Indian-made Enfield Bullets. The Bullet itself is something of an anachronism in the modern world, a motorcycle that is by all appearances a 1950s machine but that is still produced brand-new in India. The bike was conceived in the UK just after the Second World War to provide cheap and reliable transport for police forces, the royal mail, army and air force, and also as a sturdy working man's steed.

The Indian Army purchased many thousands of Bullets prior to independence in 1947. They were so successful that, post-independence, a factory was set up in Madras to produce them under licence. The Enfield India Company, now Royal Enfield Motors, has been a great success, and has steadily attempted to improve the Bullet without much changing the basic format. Today, little has changed with the bike, a testament to its ruggedness and suitability for Indian conditions.

In Goa these Bullets were available everywhere for hire and presented a cheap way of getting from happening to happening in style and convenience. Somehow or other, I managed to remain more or less upright on my hired machine, thumping noisily around the small village roads. For six glorious weeks I managed to eke out my small reserves of rupees before having to return home to a squalid squat in Wandsworth, to reminisce about India and dream of my next visit.

After the thrills and exotica of India, squat life in London seemed dull and pointless. I spent the next few years trying to get out, finally succeeding in 1980 with a job offer from Durban Snake Park in apartheid South Africa. Although I'd long had an amateur interest in reptiles, particularly snakes, and had helped out at a couple of minor zoos in England, my position as curator for the park was in some aspects way beyond my abilities. Regardless, I muddled along happily enough managing the large collection of snakes, lizards, turtles and crocodiles.

But South Africa, although a stunningly beautiful country, was controlled by a government whose policies I was unable to stomach. After a couple of years I regretfully gave up my dream job in the wrong country and headed further southward.

In New Zealand I soon discovered the thrills of sailing a small yacht around large oceans. I also met Lily, a feisty dark-haired Lebanese-New Zealander. Over the next six years Lily and I sailed around New Zealand's Hauraki Gulf and cruised the islands of Tonga and Fiji in our small yacht. During hurricane season each year we based ourselves on Great Barrier Island near Auckland, living a self-sufficient lifestyle in our small bach in the lush New Zealand bush.

Inevitably, Lily and I both turned forty. Feeling the pressure from this milestone we decided to become more responsible citizens and to give up our freewheeling lifestyle, at least for a while. A move to Waiheke Island in the inner Hauraki Gulf brought us even closer to the big city of Auckland, but still far enough away from its bustle. A small but well-timed dabble in the rapidly expanding Waiheke property market left us with enough cash to build our dream home overlooking the sea, and with a bit left over. Although we'd not often been in a surplus cash situation we knew exactly what to do with the money – spend it on a long-awaited trip back to India.

Lily had also briefly visited India in the seventies, spending most of her time in the Himalayas, so we were both very keen to return. We started poring over all the brochures, maps and other literature we could find, and decided that Rajasthan would be our destination. Soon much of our talk was of India, train timetables, and itineraries.

During our planning Rachel, one of Lily's nursing workmates, returned from an extended trip through India. Over dinner one evening Rachel and her husband Grant showed us photos that further stimulated our travel juices. Then Grant told us about the motorbike they'd used to tour around India, and took us down to his garage to actually show me the machine – they'd liked it so much they'd brought it back with them. It was an Enfield Bullet. I was almost beside myself with excitement.

As I gazed longingly at this fine machine Grant and Rachel spoke enthusiastically of their Indian friend, Lalli Singh, a Sikh motorcycle dealer who had faithfully undertaken all their motorbike preparation in the Karol Bagh district of New Delhi.

'Look him up if you get the chance, he's a really nice guy,' suggested Grant, handing me Lalli Singh's business card.

I knew then that the first thing I'd do after arriving in India would be to look up this man, and I clutched the card as though it were some treasured amulet. During the week before our departure I fingered the card again and again amidst my musing of India, motorbikes, and riding along exotic country roads. After twenty years, my dream of returning to India, and once again riding a Bullet, was about to come true.

Chapter Two

On the very first morning after arriving in New Delhi, Lily and I ventured out onto the busy streets hoping to flag down an autorickshaw. We needn't have worried. Immediately a swarm of rickshaws descended upon us. Handing Lalli Singh's well-worn business card to one of the rickshaw drivers I asked, 'How much to Karol Bagh?'

'Fifty rupees', he grunted, eyeing us speculatively.

After a bit of spirited haggling we settled on twenty rupees and, savouring our small victory, squeezed into the back of the vehicle. This space could no doubt comfortably accommodate several short, thin adults, but for our more substantial Western bodies it was like trying to fit salmon in a sardine tin. With my head pressed up against the canvas roof I had only a peephole view, but I saw more than enough pandemonium as we dodged at terrifying speed between buses and ox carts with only millimetres to spare. We caromed breathtakingly close to several large trucks, and I feared for my knees sticking out the side of our machine. As well, the tailpipes of every truck and bus seemed to be malevolently designed to belch acrid clouds of black smoke directly into the faces of defenceless rickshaw passengers. We couldn't seriously be thinking of riding a motorbike in *this*. We wouldn't last two minutes.

Our confidence in the rickshaw driver, and our hope of getting to Karol Bagh, slowly ebbed as he stopped every few kilometres to ask directions to the bike shop. Finally he pulled over at a side road and pointed.

'You out here! Shop short way only.'

Our feeble demand that he must take us the entire way for our twenty rupees had the sole effect of making him suddenly unable to understand English. Defeated, we coughed up the twenty rupees and headed off down the street. This looked promising. This was obviously the industrial part of town and, more importantly, the part of town that dealt solely with autorickshaw repairs and sales. Surely the motorbikes would be close by.

A sea of black and yellow autorickshaws spread ahead of us, all in various stages of repair and destruction. Brand-new chromium and tassled dreams rested beside rusted wrecks tipped on their sides. Mechanics swarmed over them, replacing rear axles or dismantling engines.

'Maybe we should forget the bike and buy one of these,' I joked to Lily, nodding at a particularly gaudy tinsel-fringed machine uphol-stered in red velvet and sporting an extravagantly painted and polished body. Lily's snort reminded me that we were here to look at motorbikes, not temples of bad taste masquerading as vehicles.

Spying a rickshaw owner lingering hopefully by his machine, I asked him whether he knew where we could find Abdul Aziz Road, our ultimate destination.

'No, I do not know this road. What are you wanting there?'

I explained about Mr Lalli Singh and the motorcycles.

'Ah, the motorbike bazaar is just up there, maybe two hundred yards away.'

Sure enough, a short way down the street – at an almost hidden sign pointing to the 'unknown' Abdul Aziz Road – the rickshaws gave way to rows of motorbikes and an abundance of signs advertising 'motorcycle and scooter commission agents'. Long lines of Enfields took up most of the roadway, and as we wandered amongst them my pulse quickened.

We stopped for a closer look.

'Can I help you sir?' A rotund Sikh appeared from nowhere. 'Are you seeking to purchase a motorcycle?'

'Well . . . perhaps. But really we are searching for Mr Lalli Singh, who has been recommended to us,' I replied.

'So sorry,' said the Sikh smoothly, 'but Mr Singh is now a long way from here and is no longer selling motorcycles. I am Mr Mukash and these are my motorcycles. Come and have a cup of chai and we can discuss your requirements at your leisure.'

After our harrowing rickshaw ride and wandering around the bazaar, a cup of sweet spicy tea seemed just what we needed.

'What sort of bike are you looking for, and how much were you thinking of paying?' he asked, after the chai had been served.

This was a good question. So far we had only vaguely thought about a bit of a Rajasthan tour, and perhaps a month or so in southern India. We had no idea what sort of bike to get.

He waved at a nearby bike. It was shiny enough, but oil was dripping onto the road from some mysterious leak, and its exhaust pipe looked distinctly burnt.

'This Bullet has been completely reconditioned,' he assured us. 'You could take delivery and depart tomorrow if you wished. It is only forty-eight thousand rupees.'

We were unimpressed. That, we'd been told, was the cost of a brand-new Bullet, not a leaking burnt-out one.

'What about the oil leak?'

'Oh! That is a small detail and can be remedied if you wish,' he said dismissively. 'This is a fine bike and is fully guaranteed.'

As we soon discovered, all of his bikes had 'small details' that needed to be fixed. This begged the question of what condition the internals would be in. Not so good, judging by the externals. Mr Mukash insisted that any problem would be easily solved. But we were dubious, especially when he was quite unwilling to start any of his 'fine bikes' because he had 'no batteries' or 'no petrol was available'. After thanking him for his time and hospitality and fending off his demands to make a decision then and there, we left a slightly grumpy Mr Mukash and continued on through the bazaar.

Fifty metres further along, outside a motorbike accessory shop, we came across a Dutch couple rummaging through a pile of elastic tie-downs. It looked as though these two were undertaking a similar sort of adventure to ours.

'Do you know where Lalli Singh's shop is?' we asked.

'Oh yes, he's just down that alleyway, about a hundred metres, on the corner.'

We thought a few nasty thoughts about Mr Mukash.

'Are you looking to buy an Enfield?' asked the woman.

When we told them of our plans they looked at each other and smiled.

'We're still waiting for our bike to be finished,' she said gloomily. 'We've been here ten days now, but maybe it will be ready tomorrow. You should allow at least a week to get everything organised.'

We set off in the direction they'd indicated. On the corner of the alleyway and the next road sat a tiny, three-metre-square open-fronted shop crowded with dilapidated desks and bike parts. Outside at the front was a small concrete platform about the same size but covered by a tarpaulin. Here, five or six mechanics crouched greasily over the entrails of a couple of disembowelled bikes.

This was the best bike dealer in Delhi?

'This can't be it' I murmured to Lily.

'Yes it is – look!' She pointed to a small grimy sign proclaiming 'Inder Mohan Motors Proprietor Lalli Singh'.

Approaching the shop, I enquired to the general muddle where I might find Lalli Singh.

'Yes, I am he' replied a tall slim Sikh. 'Please come in and have some chai'.

'We're friends of Grant and Rachel from New Zealand' said Lily as we sat down. After the Mr Mukash experience we were even more eager to trade on our friends' good will.

'Ah, yes' Lalli Singh gave no sign of recognition. 'How are they?'

'Both fine, and they still have the bike, which is going well'.

We sat down at the crowded desk and eyed up this calm good-looking man as he limped around the office setting out the teacups.

I whispered to Lily, 'He doesn't remember Grant or Rachel'.

She agreed. So much for using our friends for good will or good deals.

As we drank our chai, we explained our proposed trip to Lalli and asked about buying a bike.

'I have two bikes which would possibly be suitable to your requirements' he said.

Stepping outside, he pulled out a couple of bikes from the row, a very styley looking 350cc and a slightly dilapidated 500cc bike. Both were Enfield Bullets.

'The 350 is in very good condition, but if you are to be carrying much luggage with you, I think it would be better for you to have a 500 with a little extra power' he continued. 'The engine and gearbox on this 500 are in excellent condition and you will be able to fix up the appearance very easily. Why don't you take them for a test ride?'

He turned the key on the 350 and kicked it into life, then gestured to me to get on. Suddenly all my nervousness and trepidation about riding in the traffic horrors of Delhi disappeared. This was the reason I'd come to Karol Bagh. This was the reason we were in India. I was on the bike in a flash.

I cruised around the block, going through the gears and checking out the brakes. Traffic parted miraculously as I beeped the horn and wove in and out of the turmoil. What had seemed insanely dangerous was just a matter of concentration and a bit of assertive driving. I returned to the alleyway where they were both waiting.

'You should try the 500 now, but go a bit farther and get an idea of the bike's performance at speed,' suggested Lalli.

He gave me instructions on how to get to the Ridge Road, a stretch of fairly open highway. I found the road and wound the bike up to around 80 kilometres per hour. It responded sweetly, and to my surprise even felt as though it had some more in reserve. Around fifteen long, thrilling minutes later I arrived back at the shop, grinning.

'Yes, the 500 has got more power,' I agreed. 'The 350 looks a lot better though. What sort of price are you hoping to get for these bikes?'

'The 350 would be forty thousand and the 500 around thirty thousand, although you will have to spend around ten thousand on the 500 to get it fully ready for a big journey. I think if you do these things to the 500, you will have a very good bike.'

I glanced at Lily. She raised her eyebrows almost imperceptibly, our secret 'It's OK' sign.

'It seems a little expensive,' I countered, prepared to bunker down for a hard and lengthy haggle.

'I think if you are looking in the bazaar, you will not be finding a bike this good for this price. It would be very difficult for me to sell it to you any cheaper.'

It was hard to deny his logic. And there was something about the dignified attitude of this quietly spoken man we found both reassuring and disarming.

'We'll have a look around and perhaps get back to you,' said Lily, closing round one of the negotiations.

'That will be fine.' He paused. 'By the way, how is Kuri?'

'Sorry, I don't know anyone named Kuri,' I replied, a little puzzled, adding, 'kuri is the New Zealand Maori word for dog.'

'Yes, I know,' said Lalli. 'This is the name of Grant and Rachel's dog, a German shepherd. When they were visiting India last year they were very sad to be apart from him.'

'Oh!' I raised my eyebrows at Lily. 'The dog was fine when we visited them last week.'

There was obviously a lot more to Lalli Singh than met the eye.

Bidding Lalli farewell with a coy 'we might be back the next day' we headed back into the bazaar, our eyes roving across the rows of motorbikes. The variety and number of motorcycles available overloaded all our senses, and the prospect of investigating several more dealers was daunting in the sizzling-hot Delhi street. As we walked past Mr Mukash's shop he ignored us in the manner of a man caught in a lie.

I had just opened my mouth to suggest that we should just go back to Lalli's and get the 500 when Lily said suddenly, 'Sod it! We could spend a week messing around here. Let's just go back to Lalli's and get the 500.'

Within minutes of this unanimous snap decision we found ourselves back at Lalli's corner shop. Waving aside all discussion of purchasing motorbikes he invited us to join him for a lunch of bean curry and chapatis at his desk.

During lunch Lalli spun fascinating tales of some of the journeys that he'd made throughout India. It dawned on us that here was a man who not only sold and repaired bikes, but who was passionate about them as a way of seeing his country, a place he obviously loved deeply.

As he talked about forts and castles and camping in the desert, I couldn't hold myself back any more.

'We'll buy the 500!' I blurted.

'I know', Lalli smiled benignly. 'I am sure it will give you good service.'

Far from feeling we'd been done by some smooth-talking snake oil salesman, we felt confident the decision was the right one.

'Will you be taking the bike back to New Zealand after your journey? If so, it would be better to deal only with the mechanicals now and when you return from your journey, we can deal with the paint and chrome.'

The thought of riding the bike around Waiheke Island was very attractive. After some discussion about costs and shipping times, we decided that the bike would go back to New Zealand.

While Lalli set about organising the work needed on the bike, we set off to the nearest bank to change our Kiwi dollars into rupees. In exchange for our fifteen one-hundred-dollar notes we received a huge pile of fifty-rupee notes almost a foot high, all stapled together in wads of five thousand rupees. We stuffed these into every pocket and money belt we had. Still there were several stacks remaining, which we bundled under our shirts. We looked decidedly and self-consciously plumper on our way back to the shop.

Upon our return, the bike had already been moved into the work area. Several mechanics were attacking it with gusto, removing parts and handing them to a young man who squatted in the road, meticulously scrubbing and cleaning them in a wok full of kerosene. Lalli introduced the men as Imran and Alum, the mechanics, and Manali, the cleaner.

At Lalli's desk our money was duly counted and an impressive receipt, complete with a duty stamp and seal, was issued.

'What about the registration documents?' I was aware of the warning from one of the guidebooks to 'never part with your money until you have the registration papers in your hand'.

'Oh, they will be taking a couple of days to be changed into your name,' Lalli replied. 'I will send them to the agent tomorrow.'

'When will the work on the bike be complete?' I was more than a little impatient, watching Imran expertly remove the cylinder head.

'If all goes well, probably only two days or so. Come by in the morning and we will have a better idea.'

Once again we said our goodbyes, then headed towards the main street to search for an autorickshaw for the return ride to our hotel.

I reflected upon the rather sobering fact that on this, our first day in India, we had just broken every rule and gone against all the advice received and resolutions made. The majority of the funds for our trip were now securely in someone else's hands, and all we had to show for it was a scrap of paper with a stamp, albeit official-looking, on it. We had not seriously researched the value of second-hand bikes, but instead had leapt impetuously at the first thing Lalli had offered, a fairly rough-looking specimen which was now in pieces at the side of a road that we would probably have a fair bit of trouble finding again. Looking at our situation logically, it didn't look good at all. Yet I had an overwhelming feeling that it would all be fine. I was sure that our newfound friend – on precious little evidence I already looked upon him as a friend – would come through for us.

'What do you think?' I shouted to Lily over the scream of the rickshaw engine. 'Have we been had?'

'Nah. There's no deviousness in that guy's face at all. I'm sure he's straight up. Either that or he's a very good poker player.'

At six o'clock the next morning we were woken by chanting from the temple just outside our window. There was no point in waiting any longer. After an early breakfast of parathas and yoghurt, we struck a bargain with a rickshaw driver and headed to the bike shop. This time, there was no terror in the ride. This time, I was able to give directions. We arrived outside the shop at mid-morning.

Unlike our previous day's visit the street was deserted. All the rows of bikes were stored away and most of the shops shuttered and locked. We found Manali slowly awakening from his bed on the office floor. There was no one else around. Manali offered us chai and, sitting on the workshop floor, he sleepily told us in a combination of sign language and broken English that he had been in Delhi for a year. He hailed from Manali in the northern mountainous state of Himachel Pradesh and his name in Himacheli was unpronounceable to these Delhi-ites, so they'd nicknamed him Manali. Next year, he said, he would become a mechanic's helper and two years later, if all went well, he would be a fully fledged mechanic.

Perhaps in the future he would either open up a shop here in Delhi or return home to do the same.

In the meantime, he was very happy with his job and was especially happy to be the unpaid security guard for the shop, as he was able to sleep on the office floor every night and save many rupees in rent. Compared to the many indolent teenagers we knew back in New Zealand, this handsome sixteen-year-old demonstrated impressive resourcefulness in coming to what was to him a foreign land and planning a career.

As the mechanics drifted in and preparations for the day's work began, we watched the street slowly come to life. Chai and snack vendors pushed their carts through the throng of commuters, calling out to all, interested or not, that theirs were the best and hottest snacks. Most did a brisk trade with people arriving at work. The noise of the snack-wallahs was punctuated by the occasional crash of steel roller doors being slammed up, as one by one the shops of the bazaar proclaimed themselves open for business. Shopkeepers meticulously swept the areas of unpaved dirt in front of their shops, and bikes were rolled out and lined up with military precision.

A couple of hours later, still no work had begun on our bike, but at least Lalli had arrived. After greeting us he began his morning ritual. He lit incense sticks and, chanting under his breath, passed the smoke over a small shrine on his desk, then over a picture of a distinguished-looking old man who we later found out was his deceased father. He then took out a small packet of sweets, broke pieces off one of the sweets and placed these on the shrine and picture. The rest of the sweets were then shared amongst everyone in the shop, including us.

'By sharing this you share in the blessings of today,' explained Lalli.

Next, he took a small green lime and several red chillies from another packet, threaded them on a piece of cotton, and hung the strange little mobile by the door.

'This is to ward off evil spirits from the shop. They will find it too hot and bitter in here with these by the door. Now we can get down to business. Chai?'

By now, it had become obvious to us that no business could be conducted without chai. As we sipped yet another cup of the sweet tea, we pressed Lalli for word on the bike's progress.

A new front wheel was being made with better brakes, and the valve seats were being re-cut. The bike was now in a thousand pieces with only a crankcase, gearbox, and rear wheel remaining in the frame. As we spoke, the ever-busy Imran was removing the wheel.

Lalli brought us up to date. 'All the parts are being sent for repair. If all goes well they should be back this afternoon, and we can commence to reassemble the bike.'

This all sounded promising, and we felt most reassured. As we watched Imran working away at the remains of the bike, our Dutch friends from the previous day strolled in.

'I see you found him then,' said the girl. 'Did you buy a bike?'

'Yes. This one, a 500cc.' I gestured at the heap of parts next to Imran.

Their eyes widened. 'When do you expect to leave Delhi?'

'Oh, probably the day after tomorrow,' I said.

He looked at me strangely. 'Perhaps you should not expect too much in India. We have now been waiting eleven days, and *still* our bike isn't ready.'

I didn't like the sound of that. 'So what's the problem with it then?'

'Ach! Too many to name, always something more to do. At least I have not paid all the money though.'

Another wave of despair began to roll over me as I asked, 'Which bike is yours?'

'Oh, it's not here. Another shop on the next street is doing the work. We just came here to buy some luggage carriers because no one else has the good ones.'

We left them to their purchasing and headed off into the centre of Delhi to have a good look around and distract ourselves from the thoughts of dismantled Bullets. We had arranged to meet up for dinner later with a fellow Kiwi, Brett, brother of another of Lily's workmates, who was just starting work in Delhi as a tour guide.

Brett was free from his induction training with the tour company at around six o'clock, and he had recommended that we try a rooftop restaurant near the main bazaar area. After he picked us up from our hotel we headed off into the dimly lit night, without the slightest idea where we were going. The evening streets were alive with people doing their shopping, and the sidewalks, or what passed for sidewalks, overflowed with barrows offering all manner of foods displayed in attractive symmetrical piles. We crossed a main four-lane road completely gridlocked with huge trucks vying with horse, oxen and human-drawn carts to make any progress down this choking thoroughfare. The clouds of exhaust fumes limited the view to only a couple of hundred metres, giving the scene a surreal Dante-like feel.

Coming in from the pandemonium of the street, the Metropolis

Hotel felt quite fancy and plush. We wound our way up a series of steep, narrow stairways to the roof. There was no view of the surroundings from here but a cooling breeze gave the illusion of fresh air. A dirty reddish-brown moon filtered through the dense pollution haze, adding its weak light to the candles on our table. The food was good, if a little expensive, and we enjoyed a couple of hours planning our route through Rajasthan.

After dinner we stopped at a juice stand just outside the rooftop restaurant. Brett asked about the green coconuts sitting in the fridge.

'Up in the islands we used to have four or five of them a day,' I said enthusiastically. 'They're delicious.'

Lily was dubious about the quality of the refrigeration and pointed out that we were a long way from any coconut palms. Ignoring this, Brett and I ordered one each. The tops were chopped off and we gulped them down. Mine had a slightly effervescent taste but it was cool and thirst-quenching.

We strolled through the now quiet, dark streets to our hotel and settled in for a bit of television and an early night. About an hour later it was all on, or rather all out!

At what seemed like two-minute intervals I was lunging for the bathroom, explosively ejecting fiery liquid from both ends. Spasms racked my whole body, and my head felt on fire. I sat on the toilet, the only safe place, as Lily tried to get some water into my stomach. But as fast as I drank it, up it came again.

'Now I know why they put the tiles so far up the wall,' she remarked, eyeing a particularly nasty-looking deposit stuck to the wall at her eye level.

The spasms only lasted about two hours, but when they subsided

I was completely exhausted. At around three in the morning, I finally managed to get some water and a sleeping pill to remain in my stomach and blissfully passed out.

The next day we slept in through the temple chants and traffic noise. I certainly couldn't face our usual parathas for breakfast. We phoned Brett at his hotel and sure enough, he had been up all night too. We put the blame firmly on the coconut drinks. Much to her credit, Lily did not say 'I told you so'.

Later that afternoon I was feeling much better, and we again made our way to the shop, this time to find a frenzy of activity surrounding our bike. The engine was put back together, the wheels back on and Manali was painting the luggage carriers. Imran looked up at me from his work.

'Clutch very bad, new one putting.' He offered a set of burnt plates for my inspection.

'Everything else OK?' I asked hopefully.

'Yes, yes. This bike very good, no problems.'

As Imran turned back to his work, Lalli appeared holding a backrest.

'Lily will find this more comfortable on the road,' he said. 'Your bike should be ready this afternoon if all goes well.'

It certainly looked promising as Imran turned back to the clutch assembly. We joined Lalli for a chai and some advice on how to ride out of Delhi in the morning.

'I don't like the idea of riding through the south of Delhi in the rush-hour traffic,' I admitted. Even though I'd handled my first little ride on the bike well, I still didn't fancy dealing with the sort of chaos we'd seen the night before.

34

'No, it will be very busy and quite difficult for you at the start of your journey,' Lalli agreed.

He pondered us thoughtfully.

'Why don't you put the bike on the train and go down to the south of Rajasthan, maybe to Abu Road? There are some beautiful roads for biking down there. It would ease you into your journey very pleasantly.'

This seemed like excellent advice. We headed off to the station to arrange tickets and bookings.

On our way back from the ticket office we stopped at a sweet shop to pick up a box of the same Indian sweets that Lalli had offered to us in the shop the day before. These incredibly rich, bite-sized concoctions of flour, sugar, milk and spices are packaged in gaudy presentation boxes and are often exchanged between friends on auspicious occasions such as weddings and birthdays. We wanted to give them as a thank you to the men in the shop.

When we arrived back, the bike was nowhere to be seen, another having taken its place on the working platform.

'Imran has gone to the electrical shop to fit new loud horns,' said Lalli. 'He will be back soon, then everything is complete. We shall have a puja to help you on your way.'

I wasn't quite sure what a puja was, but it didn't sound too ominous. I was, though, a little concerned about the rising costs for the bike. It seemed to us that Lalli had forged ahead with all sorts of extra modifications to it without asking for our consent or even opinion. Even though backrests, loud horns and locking petrol taps all seemed reasonable and probably essential accessories, what would it all cost?

We sat silent and tense as Lalli tallied up the endlessly long columns of numbers.

Finally, he looked up at us.

'Yes, there is a discrepancy from the original quotation,' he announced.

I wasn't surprised. All that extra gear slapped on without our say-so. Couldn't we trust *any* Indian merchant?

'Yes, the original total is incorrect. I have overcharged you. I must give you back four hundred and twenty-five rupees. Or would you like to take some extra spare parts?'

Feeling more than a little abashed we opted for the spares, hoping that our relief was not too obvious. As we finalised the deal Imran roared up on our bike and tooted the horns a couple of times.

'People hearing this here horn maybe thinking big truck coming. Moving very quick!' he laughed.

With our ears still ringing, we couldn't help but agree. The Bullet looked really businesslike with its big luggage carriers and crash bars. Although the paint and chrome were a bit tatty, the engine and running gear were clean and well maintained.

Just then our Dutch friends walked in once again. Whilst admiring the bike their envy was plain. 'I wish we'd used this guy. Our bike will be ready in the morning after nearly two weeks. It's amazing that Lalli did this so quickly.'

'Don't feel too bad,' I said. 'We're as amazed as you are with the service.'

It was true. All the guidebooks to India had been unequivocal in their advice not to trust anyone. We'd gone with our gut instinct and ignored them.

Sony, Lalli's dapper foreman, appeared with incense and garlands of marigolds.

'Now we will make a puja,' Lalli said.

Work stopped in the shop as we all gathered around. Sony lit the joss sticks and, after waving the smoke over the bike, wedged them in the hand levers. The garlands of marigolds were draped over the headlight of the bike and a piece of one of our sweets was broken off and placed on the speedometer.

Sony began to sing, and we all stood around the bike listening to the chanted prayers – Hindu, Sikh, Muslim, Christian and atheist alike – each lost in their own thoughts but unified by this small ceremony.

After a few minutes of prayer the sweets were handed around. Then Manali went off down the street with the box, offering them to all the neighbours and passers-by.

Seeing my puzzlement at this gesture Lalli explained quietly, 'You have shared something sweet with all those people. Now they will have sweet thoughts about you and your journey. Good, huh?'

Standing in a narrow alleyway in Delhi on the eve of our departure, this logic seemed completely unassailable.

Chapter Three

'Don't worry Lil', we've got three hours before the train goes', I called as we asked for the umpteenth time for directions to Old Delhi Railway Station. Three hours was plenty of time – *if* we could find the Old Delhi Railway Station. The madness of riding through the narrow streets of Delhi on the bike reinforced to us the good sense of taking the bike on the train for our first trip out of the city to Abu Road in Rajasthan. We rode it, heavily loaded with bags containing what we considered to be the bare essentials for our journey, through the melee of autorickshaws, trucks, buses, and overloaded pedal rickshaws. We crept on through traffic plodding along at a camel's pace, at times so gridlocked not even the bike could squeeze through. After about forty minutes of seemingly contradictory directions, we chanced upon the huge complex of one of the biggest stations in India and the world.

The 'luggage office' was not an office at all, but a large warehouse crammed with a variety of goods tied up with strings or tape and ready to be sent to all corners of India. We joined the stream of people making their way past sacks of ground-up plastic water bottles for recycling, cases of canned ghee, tin trunks of worldly possessions, and bales of magazines and pamphlets destined for just about anywhere.

Amidst this apparent confusion sat a middle-aged silver haired babu in a white shirt and longhi. His ageing Victorian desk had a pile of ledgers upon it and a large set of scales from the same era sat next to him. He was surrounded by a number of subordinates and a couple of railway policemen in dirty brown uniforms holding sub-machine guns with flaking paint. Not knowing whether to feel reassured or menaced by the ageing guns, I put our seemingly reasonable request to the babu.

'Is it,' I asked politely, 'possible to send our motorbike on the train to Abu Road?'

An unintelligible conversation ensued between him and several of his subordinates. After a few minutes the response was, 'Sorry sir, this is not possible. This is express train and luggage is only being accepted for Ahmedabad.'

He then began to furiously ignore us and get on with the far more important matter of chatting about the cricket with the two policemen.

'When will the next train be to Abu Road that we can put the bike on?' I interrupted.

He looked up at me, surprised and irritated that I was still there.

'Ahmedabad Mail, departing day after tomorrow. There may be space on it but mail is having top priority,' was the surly response.

Panic began to rise as our carefully thought-out plans started to crumble to nothing, but I tried to keep calm as I returned to Lily who was sitting close by on our luggage.

'Well, that's that idea buggered,' I muttered, collapsing beside her. 'We can't get the bike there for a couple of days. What now?'

We looked around the warehouse, at the giant mounds of mail taking up room rightfully belonging to our bike, and at the hundreds of people milling around. How do *they* get their luggage on the train, we wondered. We looked at the luggage again. We looked at the babu.

'I don't suppose we could bribe him, could we?' suggested Lily.

Throughout all our discussions and preparatory talks about the trip, much had been made of the bribery issue. On many occasions I'd made knowledgeable statements about how everyone in a position of power in India accepts bribes and life is impossible without a little baksheesh here and there. But here we were, about to offer money to a public official flanked by a couple of armed policemen. The bravado of after-dinner chats back home seemed foolhardy in the extreme when faced with the cold hard facts of a possible baksheesh backfire and a stint in an Indian prison.

I returned to the antique desk, trying to look unconcerned, and patiently waited to be noticed. After thirty seconds or so an eyebrow was raised, and I asked, 'Is there any way we can make this thing possible?'

I raised my own eyebrows in what I thought was a subtly suggestive manner, but it was obvious that I was the centre of attention of everyone in the office.

'Sir!' came the slightly exasperated reply. 'To consign your motorcycle to Abu Road on this train would be most irregular and involve discrepancies on the part of several people. They might expect to be compensated for the great risks they would be taking on your behalf sir, and they are all like myself, poor and underpaid employees of the government.'

It was fast becoming clear that I was in the presence of a master of extracting rupees from hapless railway clients. I mentally upped the amount of baksheesh I'd originally planned on offering.

'I might be able to show my appreciation to these kind people in the form of a small gift, should things go well. What sort of gift do you think would be acceptable?'

'This is not important sir. As you like,' he replied, with a dismissive flick of the hand.

Another heated conversation in Hindi broke out. I stood there trying to hold a smile while I wondered what sort of fortune they were setting us up for. Fifteen minutes passed. One of the policemen turned to me and demanded, 'Which country?' – a question that we were to become very accustomed to over the next few years. Upon hearing my reply he grunted, 'New Zealand, hmph! Very good cricket team.'

Another fifteen minutes passed. Finally the babu turned to me.

'We must go and talk to the guard of the train because he will be having the final say in this. The train will arrive in about thirty minutes and then we can go. Fill in this form.'

The time now was quarter to two and the train was scheduled to depart at three o'clock. I threaded my way back through the crowds of passengers and porters to Lily and made my progress report. The filling in of the form gave us vast and perhaps misplaced reassurance that things were going well, though it was one of those very complex quadruplicate pieces of Indian bureaucracy that demanded to know my father's name, amongst a list of other personal details.

At quarter past two the train backed into the station. So far, so good – the forms were filled in, there really was a train. Together with the luggage supervisor, we traipsed off to receive the guard's blessing. He was a slim, balding man in his forties wearing a white suit with a short-sleeved jacket that, though surely fresh on that morning, was showing the signs of having been exposed to the Delhi atmosphere. Initially, he was completely uninterested in our problem, busily supervising the loading of general cargo in one of the two cages in his luggage van.

'Luggage on this train is only possible for destination Ahmedabad,' he snapped. 'This cage must be sealed and it is a criminal offence for anyone to open it anywhere else.'

To prove his point, he slammed the door of the cage shut. One of his crew who carried a small charcoal stove heating a pot of molten wax deftly wired the gate shut. He then covered the wire with wax and stamped it with a very official-looking seal.

'You see,' explained the guard, with not a little triumph, 'all the luggage is sealed.'

I climbed into the van and looked into the second cage. 'Is this one also to be filled?'

Another loud and unintelligible discussion broke out with much gesticulation and shouting. We began to feel that the babu was an old friend, as he was obviously trying to convince the guard to put the bike on.

'You must get the permission of the station operations manager before I authorise this,' said the guard.

By now the clock was inexorably ticking, with only twenty minutes remaining before departure. Lily set off to search for and claim our reserved and non-refundable seats and I followed an assistant towards the manager's office, wondering how many more people would be making final decisions on final decisions. The office turned out to be at the other end of Platform twenty-four. We were on Platform two, and by the time we arrived at Platform twenty-four I was starting to worry about even getting back in time, let alone putting the bike on the train.

The office was a huge, grimy room almost filled by four desks arranged in a square. Four men in their shirtsleeves were playing cards on this enormous surface, having to flick their cards into the middle and stretch out with their feet off the ground to retrieve them. My plight was explained to them by the assistant to the assistant luggage supervisor.

The manager looked up at me, smiled and said, 'Your team is doing very well this year, but not so well as when Sir Richard Hadlee played for you.'

I silently counted to five and replied, 'No, we'll probably not do that well for a long time. I see that India is also doing fairly well.'

Having no idea how India was doing, I hoped that they hadn't just been thrashed by their arch-rivals Pakistan, and made a mental note to take more interest in cricket in future.

I forged ahead. 'Do you think it will be possible to get our motorcycle shipped to Abu Road on this train?'

'Of course sir,' was the astonishing reply. 'This is no problem but you must hurry, the train is leaving soon!'

'Could you please ring the luggage office to let them know?' I asked, heading towards the door.

'I would love to oblige you sir, but the station telephone system is not working. Next time you come to Delhi, you must join us for chai and a game of cards, but you must hurry now!'

We almost broke into a run on the way back to the train with only five minutes left before departure. How are we going to get the bike on in time, I asked myself.

Then, in the distance, I saw four porters lifting the Bullet into the second cage. Some magical psychic message must have been sent from the manager's office to let them know it was OK. By the time I arrived at the train, the cage was sealed for Abu Road and a crowd of expectant railway employees stood smiling around the guard van.

Ah, here came the 'gift' crunch. I drew the babu aside and put my hand in my pocket, preparing for the worst.

'The guard is being a very greedy man', he said, looking darkly in his direction. 'He is demanding twenty rupees' payment.'

Twenty rupees. One dollar!

'Well', I replied, struggling to mask my relief and not burst into hysterical laughter, 'I suppose I have no option but to pay him.'

'Then there is the small matter of the two policemen and myself, sir', the babu continued.

We agreed upon a total of forty-five rupees to cover everyone. I pulled out a fifty-rupee note and handed it to him.

'Apologies, sir, but I have no change with me, I will go back to the office.'

The time now was one minute before three. There was no time to go to the office, a distant 250 metres away, and I was starting to edge towards our compartment in the opposite direction. We pushed through the crowds of people farewelling their friends and families, but he was obviously unhappy with the change situation and was going through his pockets counting out coins. As we reached our compartment, he was still glumly struggling with the coins. I took pity and pointed to a legless beggar sitting on the platform.

'Give the change to that man from both of us', I suggested, doubtful the beggar would ever see a single rupee. The babu's face broke into a wide smile as I got onto the train and shook his hand.

'You are a very generous man. Good luck', he said.

'In the cricket?' I replied, having learnt a thing or two that afternoon.

'No! On your journey of course.'

This whole two-and-a-half hour theatrical production had been eked out with the sole purpose of extracting the princely sum of two dollars fifty from us. Surely not, I thought as I walked down the corridor of the train. They can't be that desperate for a couple of bucks. Split between them it amounted to fifty cents each. It had been fairly entertaining though – thank god I hadn't spat the dummy. Now that would have been entertaining for them!

Entertaining. Yes. With the bike, and us, safely on the train, I replayed the afternoon's events. Had I imagined some barely concealed smiles and signalling eyebrows over the past few hours? I began to understand the truth – these characters had been having a bit of afternoon sport with us. Unlike in the West, where we shun controversy and confrontation, here it is relished as a part of everyday life, but to lose one's temper indicates a lack of control and weakness of character. At least we'd acquitted ourselves without complete shame but it must have been fairly amusing for them to watch us hanging on to control. I reached my seat and collapsed beside Lily, slightly shell-shocked.

As the train slowly pulled away, we stared out the window. Our last view of Old Delhi Station was of the babu handing my fifty-rupee note to the legless beggar.

Several hours later, the sleeping-car attendant shook me awake, calling out 'Abu Road in ten minutes.'

Lily and I staggered out of our berths immediately alert, but tense and uneasy about our prospects of actually taking possession of our bike. Our sleeping compartment was near the front of the train. Our bike was an entire ten carriages back. 'When the train stops, you stick with the bags and I'll run down and get the bike off,' I said to Lily.

I stepped outside our air-conditioned compartment into the stifling corridor at the end of the carriage, where several smokers were indulging by the open doors. Beyond them the early morning blackness clattered by as I wondered what dramas awaited us in Abu Road, once the train finally stopped. It was too much to hope that there wouldn't be any.

'You are alighting here?' asked one of the smokers.

'Yes,' I replied. 'How far to go?'

'Only a short time now. You must be very quick here because the train is stopping only three minutes,' he solemnly advised.

This wasn't welcome news. I couldn't bring myself to tell him about our bike sitting at the rear of the train.

As we drew nearer the station Lily and I organised our bags and helmets, then moved to the corridor and positioned ourselves by the door.

'Ah, you are motorcycling, I see,' commented the ever-helpful smoker. 'Be careful, it is very dangerous on the roads in India. Where is your motorcycle?'

The screech of the train's brakes drowned out my terse reply.

Before the train had even stopped we'd jumped onto the platform. Once the bags had been tossed off the train I sprinted, or tried to sprint, through the milling crowd of passengers meeting and greeting well-wishers, chai-wallahs, porters and general hangers-around.

I'll never make it, I thought as I pushed through the morass past the fifth car from ours, with five more to go. Then four to go. Then three.

Then, the train horn sounded. Slowly, the train started to move.

'SHIT, SHIT, SHIT!' I exclaimed to the world. There was no use trying to make it now. I stopped running. When I looked up, it was into a circle of faces, amazed at the antics of the crazy foreigner. At this point I was beyond caring what anyone thought. All I could see was the train moving off into the distance, leaving us behind and taking our bike with it.

As I was considering what to do next, I noticed some commotion just beyond my audience. It was a uniformed clerk shouting out to all in front of him what I presumed to be 'Get out of the way!'

As people got out of the way, I could see what all the fuss was about.

There were two porters, pushing our bike towards the luggage office.

I wasted no time in rushing over to the clerk and introducing myself as the owner of the bike. Lily joined us with the luggage as the clerk began to enter the bike's and our details in his many ledgers. His desk sat in the fenced-off parcels area of the station surrounded by a high chain-link barrier. Bystanders pressed up against the mesh in a solid mass, ardently watching every detail of the proceedings. Weak orange lights shed a dim glow, just enough to see where we were going but little else. It was like being on the set of a very low-budget movie.

'We have received a special telegraph from Delhi regarding your motorcycle,' announced the clerk, flourishing the dingy piece of paper. 'It says "Highest priority. Please to be off-loading one piece motorcycle arriving on Ahmedabad Express and offer all assistance to said motorcycle's owner Mr Steve, son of Andreij from New Zealand." I am your servant sir, and my office is at your disposal,' he smiled, gesturing at the cluttered desk and bowing.

I was hugely surprised. I hadn't expected such enormous results from our little bribe in Delhi. I'd half expected to have to go through the whole baksheesh process again.

'Is it possible to prepare the bike here?' I asked.

47

'But of course! Do you require a mechanic? My cousin in the next village is an A1 Enfield mechanic – perhaps you should get him to service your bike before setting off,' he offered hopefully.

'No, no, thank you. It's been serviced already. We just want to take off the packaging and put on the mirrors and luggage.'

'No problem sir. Feel free to use this space here,' he said.

We began tearing off the cardboard protecting the bike and rummaging for the mirrors, petrol and elastic tie-down cords out of our luggage – but casually, as though we off-loaded motorcycles from trains and stuck them back together all the time. From beyond the fence the crowd of onlookers discussed our every action, occasionally calling out questions – 'Where are you coming from?' 'Where are you going?' As I fiddled with spanners and mirrors, Lily went off to find a cup of tea. A few moments later she returned with a chai-wallah, who brought his mobile stand complete with smoke-belching kerosene stove into the parcels office. We ordered tea for all the staff at a total cost of around fifty cents.

By this time we were all becoming good friends. Several of the workers standing around tried to help me secure our luggage onto the bike, but they only managed to get totally in the way. Even though this was a bit annoying, it was hard to resist their friendly efforts to help. Besides, we had another hour to wait until dawn and we'd been strongly advised against riding in the dark.

After a bit of obligatory cricketing conversation and another round of chais, grey light slowly began to filter into the station. Dawn had arrived. This was it, the start of our first ride in India. There remained no option but to take several deep breaths, cross our fingers and get on our bike. We shook hands all around and, with promises to return soon, started the motor and chugged out of the station.

Sony performs the puja at Bharatpur.

Lily and Steve give a friend a ride.

KAREN GOA

Left
Imran Khan, the mechanic, at work as usual.

Below
Gopal Bhavan Palace, Deeg.

Opposite
Lalli Singh and his wife, Neelam, in traditional finery at their wedding.

KAREN GOA

RAVI CHAUHAN

Left
A woodcutter and his 'catch'.

Below
The elusive tiger at Ranthambhore National Park.

STEVE KRZYSTYNIAK

DAVID HUNTER

As we wound our way around the potholes of the still-sleeping town, our nervousness at being on the road for our very first ride began to subside. The town faded away as we turned onto an almost empty two-lane road and picked up the pace. Huge neem and baobab trees lined the highway, and there was an otherworldly quality to the light.

An old turbaned man bicycling towards us out of the faint wisps of morning mist stopped and stared as we approached, then smiled and waved.

'The natives are friendly,' I called out over my shoulder.

A road sign indicated 'Mount Abu 25'. We turned off, heading uphill on a narrower road. A wide, fertile green valley opened up on our right. The bike chugged merrily up the hill in third gear, and it seemed as relieved as we were to finally be on the road. As we climbed higher, we passed several shrines and temples clinging to the hillside. Sadhus performed their morning devotions kneeling in front of their idols. Gangs of marauding monkeys lounged across the road playing chicken with the traffic, turning to snarl at us before leaping out of our way at the last possible minute. Near the top of the climb a small chai stand stood at a hairpin bend overlooking a vast flat plain. It looked like a good place for our first rest stop.

As we dismounted, we noticed a couple of camel drivers urging their reclining beasts of burden to stand up. The camels struggled to regain their feet under the weight of four canvas sacks – full of what, it was impossible to say – roped onto their backs. In their traditional Rajasthani dress of white jodhpurs, loose cotton shirts and outsized electric-green turbans, the two camel drivers seemed exotic and wild, and we couldn't help staring. As we removed our helmets to reveal the pale faces beneath, the two Rajasthanis turned and stared back at us, jaws dropping in equal amazement.

For several moments all four of us stared, mouths agape at these alien visions. Then we all burst out laughing. We waved our goodbyes, and they headed off down the road behind their two heavily laden camels. The mist had burnt off, and the view of patchwork fields below us stretched for ten kilometres or more.

'We'll be riding across that in a few days,' I said to Lily. In our short ride up the hill we'd already had more glimpses of Rajasthani life than we'd ever expected. What lay ahead certainly looked inviting.

Chapter Four

Over the next three months our introduction to India was one that few travellers could hope to experience. After gently easing ourselves into the tourist-friendly towns of Mt Abu and Udaipur and enjoying their comforts, we set out to tentatively explore the back roads in southern Rajasthan, avoiding the well-trodden travellers' circuit. Armed with an atlas and a tattered road map we visited small villages that rarely, if ever, saw any Western visitors. We rode our Bullet along many roads depicted by a single faint line on the map. Some of these rattled our bones and seriously shook up the Bullet, but many of the worst roads led to some of the most fascinating places.

The Bullet was more than up to the task we demanded, though, and over the weeks we both developed an enormous respect for this primitive but rugged motorcycle. Everywhere we stopped a crowd formed, and we'd quickly be surrounded by inquisitive villagers. The sight of two Westerners on a motorbike was so completely outside their experience that we might have just landed from outer space, but their friendliness and generosity never ceased to astound us.

One of many instances of this hospitality occurred when, on the narrow road from Lalslot to Dhausa, our lack of preparation for foul weather landed us nowhere near any decent-sized town and about to get very wet. A bearded man sheltering under a small lean-to roof by the roadside waved us over. By now the rain had changed from a mere shower to a deluge and we were becoming uncomfortably soaked, so we rode in under the roof, parked and made our smiling introductions.

As always, everyone from miles around hurried over to see what all the fuss was about. Within minutes we were surrounded by almost a hundred smiling villagers, many of them children, all chattering animatedly and obviously discussing every aspect of our appearance in great detail. No one spoke much English, and they were all surprised at our ignorance of Hindi, a foreign language to them but the lingua franca of all the rest of India as far as they were concerned.

'From Delhi?' one of them asked.

'Nahin, nahin, New Zealand', we replied.

'Ah, Switzerland! Many mountains. Barber shop in village having poster on wall.'

'Nahin, nahin, **New Zealand!!** Richard Hadlee!'

Once more, our point of contact was cricket. These people from a small village in the middle of nowhere knew more about our national team than we did, but we tried our best to seem not completely ignorant.

The small building where we'd stopped was a village health centre, and the lean-to alongside held a small carpentry business. The carpenter showed us his pride and joy, a table saw and planer with which he turned out crude but strong doors and chairs. Piles of chair legs and backs awaited assembly nearby.

'Very sorry, machine not working. No electricity.'

'When will the electricity resume?' I asked.

'Oh, maybe evening time or tomorrow,' was the casual reply.

Supplying power to rural areas has supposedly been a government priority for a number of years, but when it arrives in these remote villages it certainly isn't reliable. But to these villagers some power, however erratic, was better than none at all.

After we'd shared a cup of tea, Raj, the paramedic, arrived on his moped, water dripping from his raincoat.

'Welcome, welcome,' he cried, as we went through the introduction ritual once again. Raj, however, spoke excellent English. On finding that Lily was a nurse, he took us on a protracted tour of the medical room and asked Lily's opinion of the drugs and sparse equipment.

'Most of these are well out of date,' she said, rummaging through the boxes of antibiotics and hypertension medication.

'Yes, but it is all we have here. Villages are very low priority for drugs I'm afraid.'

Although we'd waited for nearly an hour the rain continued its steady downpour, and we were getting a little impatient to resume our journey.

'Hills are fifteen kilometres away, just before Dhausa and not raining on other side,' said Raj.

'It'll stop raining here soon though?' I asked hopefully.

'Yes, maybe tomorrow stopping rain.'

'But we have to get to Bharatpur tonight,' Lily said.

'Only short road to Dhausa, then no rain,' reiterated Raj. 'Most assuredly no rain in Dhausa. Here. You should take my jacket to keep you dry.'

He held out his jacket, a cheap, well-worn but large vinyl waterproof.

Caught entirely by surprise, I declined. 'Do you have another jacket?' I asked him.

'Oh no, but you must take it,' he insisted. 'It is an honour to help visitors to our great country.'

Raj pressed the jacket on us. I tried all sorts of polite tactics to refuse it, or at least to pay for it, but he was having none of it. Defeated, we took down his address and promised to post the jacket back. Stretched over both of us it would give a little protection from the deluge. We sat on the bike and wrapped the jacket around both of us, with my arms stuck through the sleeves.

I waved our farewells and we rode off into the torrential rain, feeling quite subdued and thoughtful. Raj, who earned far less in a year than either of us had paid for our airplane tickets to India, was willing – in fact demanded – to part with his only waterproof jacket as a gift to a couple of strangers. This was generosity on a scale we'd never experienced before, but would come to see more and more often as we travelled through India.

As we continued on, visibility dropped to less than 100 metres and at least half the road was under water. We kept our speed down to 30 kilometres per hour as we picked our way through the waterlogged potholes. About 10 kilometres down the road an Ambassador car travelling at about 80 kilometres per hour overtook us, swerving frighteningly close and spraying us with muddy water.

'This is insane,' I called to Lily.

'Let's get to Dhausa and find somewhere to stay,' she replied.

We pushed on, squinting through the rain, up along a windy hill road, and through a narrow pass. As we descended, the rain stopped as suddenly as if a tap had been turned off. The sun broke through the clouds and the road began to steam.

A few moments later we came across the lunatic Ambassador

lying drunkenly at a forty-five degree angle in an open drain. The driver had obviously mistaken the water-filled open drain for just another puddle. He and his passengers stood amongst a crowd of gesticulating villagers. We waved as we passed, trying – but not very hard – not to look too smug.

'Raj was right about the hills and the rain,' I remarked as we stopped and took off the tent jacket.

'Yep, they've obviously had plenty of practice with weather forecasting there,' agreed Lily.

The rain, however, had put us off schedule. It was now mid afternoon, and according to our map we still had 120 kilometres to cover. At our present rate of progress this would take another six long hours or so.

We asked directions in Dhausa town both to any local hotels and to the road to Bharatpur. There were, it seemed, no hotels in Dhausa, but we were asssured it was only two hours to Bharatpur.

'Sure, it's only two hours if you're in a speeding Ambassador and ready to die,' I muttered.

We set off, crossing our fingers that the Bullet's as-yet untested headlights would work if we got caught out after dark.

After we left the town the road widened from the usual narrow, snaking lanes, and we found ourselves on an almost traffic-free, two-lane highway. We were able to whiz along easily at 80 kilometres per hour. The frequent villages and towns still tossed up all sorts of hazards but, two hours later, as predicted, we arrived at Bharatpur, dry and exhilarated.

We spent a few restful days in Bharatpur, enjoying several dawn walks through the peaceful bird park and talking about our ride through Rajasthan on the Bullet. But we couldn't delay our inevitable departure forever. Eventually, we set out once more onto the traffic-clogged main highway for the last part of our journey, the 200-kilometre ride back to Delhi.

Our safe arrival back at Lalli's bike shop was like a homecoming, with familiar faces greeting us, and the sound of English once again. Lalli welcomed us with the ubiquitous chai.

'How did you enjoy your trip?'

Enthusiastically we relived some of the highs and lows of our past three months. Also sitting in the small office were an English couple who were preparing a bike for their own similar trip. They listened, rapt, hanging on our every word, asking numerous questions and casting admiring glances at our dusty, road-worn bike. 'How were the hotels? What about the roads? How did you deal with the traffic?' We dispensed advice and information like veteran riders, filling in extra details from Lily's neatly kept journal. We assured them that we'd had absolutely no problems with the bike, mainly due to good preparation and some daily preventative maintenance whilst on the road.

'You just need to spend half an hour or so after each ride tightening up all the nuts and bolts that may have loosened, and keep an eye on your fuel filter and points,' I told them, advice that we'd followed and which had served us well.

This would be our last night in India. We were flying home to New Zealand the next evening; the Bullet would follow by ship. We spent the rest of the afternoon painstakingly working out the details for finishing the work on our well-used and now much-loved Bullet and shipping it back to New Zealand. After satisfying ourselves that all was complete, Lily and I invited Lalli to come along with us to a restaurant that evening. Instead, he insisted we join him and his family at his mother's house for dinner.

It was well into the evening when we finally left Manali to close up the shop and jumped into Lalli's tiny, borrowed Maruti car. As we inched through the rush-hour traffic to his mother's house 15 kilometres away, we mentioned that we hadn't had time to see nearly enough of Rajasthan, let alone the rest of India.

'Perhaps we'll get back again next year to visit some other places, maybe Gujarat and Tamil Nadu,' I mused, unconvincingly.

Lalli glanced at me. 'You know, if you brought a few more people from New Zealand with you, perhaps they would be willing to pay some of your expenses for your next trip. You both know what to expect on the road here now. I think you could guide them really well.'

I laughed. What a ridiculous, preposterous idea! 'Us! You're kidding! We were lost most of the time ourselves!'

Lalli didn't think so. He knew an Australian who'd ridden a motorbike to the Himalayas through Leh and Ladakh a couple of years previously. This Aussie adventurer had now turned tour guide, and he returned every June with groups of paying customers who rented bikes from Lalli.

It seemed pretty far-fetched. I couldn't imagine how we would find anyone insane or foolish enough to actually pay to come to India with us on a guided trip. We dismissed the idea without a second thought.

As we crawled down the street, one of the reasons for the almost stationary traffic became apparent. The road crossed a busy commuter railway track just ahead, and the trains at this hour were so frequent that the barrier arms stayed down more than up.

'You know, almost every time we came to a train crossing on our journey in Rajasthan, the barrier was down as a train went past,' remarked Lily as we stopped just in front of the tracks.

'Well yes, this is what you should expect after putting the bike on a train,' responded Lalli, seemingly puzzled. 'There is surely a karmic consequence for each action we make.'

Till now, my perception of the concept of karma had been highly cynical. I'd heard many 'alternative' Westerners use karma as a glib way of saying 'serves you right'. But the karma Lalli referred to was not some external theoretical concept, but a part of life as commonplace as breathing.

Eventually we arrived in a relatively quiet and affluent suburb. Mrs Singh ushered us into the sitting room of her spotless home and sat us down in front of platters heaped with dried fruits and nuts. As we nibbled we chatted with Sonya, Lalli's sister.

Sonya and her husband epitomised modern India. Together they ran a small website development company. We were astonished to hear that information technology was one of India's greatest export growth areas, with many thousands of Indian computer experts doing contract work in the industrialised world and a huge software development industry thriving at home. The India that Sonya lived in and described with such energy and optimism contrasted dramatically with the rural lifestyles we'd witnessed whilst touring.

Lalli's mother called us into the dining area to sit around a table near-collapsing under the weight of numerous vegetable and rice dishes. It was a little surprising to see several meat dishes laid out as well.

'Aren't all Sikhs vegetarian?'

'Oh yes, we are most certainly vegetarians. But I thought you might like some chicken and lamb, so I made this especially,' she said smiling.

Her matter-of-fact attitude to serving her guests dishes that were forbidden to her was a pleasant contrast to some of the 'vegetarian fascists' we'd known at home. Although we had remained more or less vegetarian whilst in India, it seemed ungracious not to partake of this delicious food she'd gone to so much trouble to prepare.

Eventually we could eat no more, and she cleared the table of our plates. Lalli and his brother-in-law adjourned to the front room. I remained at the table chatting with Lily and Sonya, but sensed a slight uneasiness amongst the women. This became a physical discomfort when Lily briskly kicked me under the table and rolled her eyes towards the front room. Somewhat belatedly I got the message and excused myself to join the other two men. Almost immediately, Mrs Singh slipped through the door to sit down at the table and finally serve herself. Lalli explained to me that his mother was of the 'old school' and would not be comfortable sitting with a male guest.

At around midnight we squeezed our somewhat fatter selves back into the tiny car and drove through surprisingly empty streets back to our hotel. As we passed the Gurdwarwa Sikh temple Lalli commented, 'This is a very famous temple. The best time to see the temple is in the early morning when the Granth Sahib, our holy book, is brought out.'

'I'd love to see that one day,' I mumbled. My eyes drooped after the long day's drive and I longed to lie down and sleep. When we arrived at the hotel we banged on the door to wake the drowsy night manager and said our good nights to Lalli, promising to see him in the morning. We were in our room and asleep within five minutes.

What seemed like mere moments later, the phone in our room screeched us awake.

'Mr Singh is here for you sir,' came the grumpy night manager's voice.

'Mr Singh? Oh. Okay, I'll come down.'

I looked at the clock. Three-thirty in the morning. What could have happened to bring Lalli out at this hour? Not knowing what to expect, and fearing some catastrophe, I pulled on a pair of jeans and t-shirt and staggered downstairs. Lalli stood in the reception area, dressed impeccably in a striking white Kurta pyjama suit and turban, the Indian equivalent of his Sunday best.

'We must hurry to the temple,' he urged. 'The Granth Sahib will be taken out in half an hour. Is Lily getting ready?'

I tried to hide my complete astonishment at being woken at such an uncivilised hour of the dawn to go sightseeing. It seemed that, despite our efforts over the last three months to get to know the customs and cultures of India and its people, we still had a long way to go to getting it right.

Lily, I was sure, still lay in bed snoring. Offering to go up and hurry her along, I went back upstairs and shook her awake.

'Wassup?' she muttered from beneath the sheets.

'It looks like we're about to go for an early morning religious experience.'

I snatched the sheets off her and struggled into my smartest clothes. Minutes later we were back into the car, still partly stupified.

At this hour the streets were truly empty. It took but a few minutes to reach the temple and join the hundreds of people streaming in for the ceremony. After removing our shoes and borrowing head coverings we entered the magnificent main chamber, where three chanting priests were performing the ritual unwrapping of the holy book. We found a spot to sit at the edge of the crowd of hundreds of men and women sitting, praying and watching the scene unfold. The huge, ornate volume was slowly extracted from the gold and silver embroidered cloths, and one of the priests began to read from it. After the chill of the walk from the car park, the warmth of the temple, the monotonous chanting and the soft rug-strewn floor made sleep irresistible, and I dozed off. A few minutes later, Lily nudged me and I wakened with a start. I'd missed the most important part. It was time to go.

I walked back to the car, still half asleep, the ritual of the holy book fuzzy in my mind. It didn't seem possible that this could be our last look at India. Whether it was madness brought on by sleep deprivation, or something else, I turned to Lily.

'What do you think, Lil – about bringing a tour?'

'Well . . .' she hesitated, but only slightly. 'It's not that stupid an idea. Is it?'

As we talked over a breakfast of puri breads, chickpea curry and yoghurt in a small sweet shop, the idea of a tour slowly took shape, and grew. Lalli reminded us that the English couple in his shop seemed to think we knew a lot about India, so why wouldn't other people? We slowly developed a plan, working out the logistics of bringing a few people from New Zealand, perhaps three or four, on a bike tour. Would we make any money or even recoup our own costs? The thought of showing this extraordinary country to a small group of New Zealanders was very seductive. It was clear to us that the only way to really see India was by motorbike, to miss out most of the hassles of train and bus transport and give the true independence to stop when and where we pleased.

Would we be able to convince enough people of this? No firm decision had yet been made to start a tour. Lily and I had not sat down and asked ourselves, 'Do we want to do this? Can it be done?' But in the wee hours of that morning, it seemed not only feasible, but inevitable.

We farewelled our good friend Lalli for the last time, and strolled back to our hotel. It was six o'clock, and the city still slept. With no hawkers or rickshaws or trucks to hide the dirtiness and squalor, the back streets of Delhi looked a disgusting, rubbish-strewn mess. All of a sudden reality got a very firm grip. It was lunacy to think of coming back here. Three months of this mayhem, dirt and aggravation was enough for anyone. Our brave plan for a tour dwindled as we picked our way through the debris.

I lay in bed, savouring thoughts of the clean aeroplane and the neatly presented if somewhat tasteless meals on our flight out of India, and the comparative orderliness of our life waiting for us in New Zealand. I thought of roads without cows and mad truck drivers, streets without rubbish, cafés with cappuccino and clean toilets.

But Lalli's idea of bringing a tour group back to India wouldn't leave me alone. However ludicrous, irrational and impossible it might be, I couldn't stop thinking about it. The people and places we'd seen over the past months unspooled like a movie through my head, as I imagined leading a group of Westerners on bikes through cities and over green hills and past temples. I rolled around and around, trying to push the thought out of my mind.

But I got very little sleep. When the plane left the runway that evening, and I gazed through the window at the hazy streetlights of the Delhi evening, I was certain we'd be back.

Chapter Five

'Is everybody here?' I called out to the group, once again trying to count off heads as they milled around the hotel car park at Bharatpur.

I looked over this, our seventh group, as they gathered around their bikes waiting for the puja ceremony to begin. Even though Lily and I had already done several tours, and by now considered ourselves fairly established, I still couldn't believe we'd progressed this far from our first apprehensive foray on our very first Bullet.

Arriving home from Delhi after our first motorbike trip I'd thought, and even hoped, that when we got back to our sleepy little village on Waiheke Island the idea of taking motorbike tours through Rajasthan would die a natural death. We chatted about the tour concept amongst our friends and, far from being told we were absolutely insane and should be locked up, the response was overwhelmingly positive. Spurred on by our desire to return to India, I spent many hours with a good friend who was a wizard graphics designer as we wrote and laid out a brochure. We contacted travel agents and airlines to help us plan itineraries. I sent the brochures out to radio stations, bike shops and clubs, and to anyone I thought could spread the word.

And then we waited. And waited.

A couple of months later we'd had little response – two bookings

– to the mail-outs or any of our promotions. As weeks went by we became increasingly despondent, even privately admitting to ourselves that the whole idea might never get off the ground.

Then, completely out of the blue, a producer from New Zealand's National Radio called, asking if I would be willing to do a telephone interview about our upcoming Rajasthan tour on their afternoon programme.

I'd never been interviewed for anything before. The thought of talking about our business on National Radio terrified me more than the prospect of taking clients on bikes through Rajasthan. But it was too good an opportunity to miss. Within seconds of hanging up from this nail-biting interview, the phone started ringing and has never, to this day, stopped. Four years on Lily and I now have new identities as the owners, operators and tour leaders of *Indian Motorcycle Adventures*.

That first puja in Lalli's shop had impressed us, and we were sure it'd brought us good luck on our first ride. Lalli had also been fairly insistent that we continue the practice for our clients and always sent Sony down to Bharatpur for the ceremony. With everybody looking on, Sony pressed sticks of incense in the handlebars, and the scent of sandalwood drifted through the afternoon haze. Fresh garlands of marigolds and roses were draped over each of the Bullet motorcycles sitting in a shiny line, and around their riders' necks. The friendly face of Ganesh, the Hindu elephant god of good luck, smiled up from gaudy stickers on every motorcycle helmet and petrol tank.

For several minutes Sony chanted away in Hindi, eyes closed, and although we had no idea of the content of the prayers the feeling was very positive indeed. The chants came to a close and he opened his eyes, smiling.

'Welcome in India and all have a happy safe journey,' he said as he handed around sweets from a box.

The motorcycles and riders had been blessed. Now we could start the tour.

As the bikers organised their helmets, gloves, cameras and other touring paraphernalia for their own first ride, I stood back and cast my eye over them, searching for a potential 'problem child'.

I was pretty sure it wouldn't be Alex, with his infectious guffaw and a luxuriant white moustache. He'd been riding motorcycles practically all his life. Or Jeanine, a commercial pilot who flew small aircraft around the Hauraki Gulf for Waiheke Air Service. The previous year she and a friend had ridden 1800 kilometres around the South Island of New Zealand on their pink 50cc scooters. Both of these riders were in their sixties, and while age didn't always mean wisdom, I thought it probably applied to these two.

Ken, a youthful forty-something boatbuilder, and his writer wife Karen riding pillion were Canadians living in Auckland and, if they lived up to the Canadian reputation for being law-abiding citizens, could probably be counted on to do the safe thing. Easy-going Owen, a property consultant around the same age as Ken and Karen, didn't seem like the panicky kind. Also, he had the advantage of having his own Enfield Bullet to ride around at home and was already familiar with their eccentricities. The farming brothers Brian and Neil, in their fifties, had left their farms on many occasions to do some lengthy road trips in New Zealand and Australia, and they looked controlled and very comfortable on the Bullets as they waited for the others to get ready.

That left Matt and Warren. Even though Matt was the 'baby' of the group by at least a decade, the thoughtful maturity of this young advertising copywriter gave me more confidence than I felt when I talked to Warren, who was a good fifteen years older. Although Warren claimed many years' riding experience, he looked nervous on the bike. Even this early in the trip he was a bit of a lone wolf, and I hoped I wouldn't have trouble getting him to stick with the group.

Overall though, I had a good feeling about this lot. From listening to their conversations last night, they were mostly experienced bikers and were under no illusions about the conditions that faced them.

Once I'd finished my little assessment I kicked my bike into life as a signal to the rest of the group. With varying degrees of success, each rider tried to start their own bike. Imran, keenly perceptive as always, materialised like a genie at the side of bikers who were already struggling with their machine's unaccustomed quirks. He rushed back and forth, helping to start flooded engines and flipping kill switches left turned off or petrol taps closed. He glanced at me and raised his eyebrows. We both chuckled, knowing that within a week most if not all of this bunch would be riding like seasoned veterans.

This, though, was always the risky part of any tour. Getting the bikers to stick to around the same speed on the same bit of road without getting lost, confused, or worse was always a challenge, to say the least. The problem was, of course, that an abundance of distractions hurled themselves at these bikers virgin to Indian roads, all vying to drag their attention away from the road just long enough to cause an accident.

With this in mind, we took each group for its first outing on a short ride along the relatively untravelled road to the small town of Deeg, to try to ease them into the Indian traffic as painlessly as possible. Over the years our minor spills had almost always been on this first part of the tour, as the riders got to grips with their bikes and the traffic. The reward at the end of the 30-kilometre ride was a tour of the Gopal Bhavan Palace, one of the most beautiful and least-visited palaces in India.

As we pulled out of the hotel entrance, I kept the speed down. Lily stood up on the rear pegs and turned around to count the bikes and make sure everyone was still with us.

'Yep! I can see the Sumo now. Let's go,' she said.

The great advantage of having the Sumo as a backup vehicle was that, when we could see it at the rear of our snake of bikes, we could pretty safely assume that all were present and accounted for. Ratan's primary directive was that he should never overtake any of our bikes, and he stuck to this rule religiously.

All the bikes needed to be refuelled before setting off on the main road, so we stopped at a petrol pump on the edge of Bharatpur town. As we pulled in Lily jumped off to direct the bikes, signalling wildly like a traffic cop. The fuelling process always attracted a large crowd of curious locals. One by one the bikes were lined up and rolled forward to be filled, with the fuel meter running continuously. Every now and then, an opportunistic Indian on a scooter or bike tried to push into the line, perhaps hoping for a free tankful.

'Keep an eye on your stuff,' I cautioned, as I spied gloves, helmets, and day packs on bike seats or lying around untended by their owners. The crowd of spectators now numbered in the hundreds and, although we had never had a significant theft, there was no reason to tempt fate on the first day.

The fuel pumped and paid for, I gathered everyone around.

'OK folks, we head along this street for half a kilometre, straight at the first junction then left at the next. About six kilometres past that there's a railway crossing, and we'll all stop on the other side to regroup. Be careful, and remember to use your horns!'

The bikes were started again and, horns blaring for practice as much as anything else, we picked our way out of the dense crowd and onto the busy street. Moments later, Warren stalled his bike in the middle of a throng of carts and trucks. There were some frayed nerves as he tried to restart his Bullet in a rush to avoid what he no doubt thought would be certain crushing in the traffic.

But unlike Western drivers none of the Indian drivers behind honked their horns impatiently, shook their fists or yelled obscenities. The traffic merely parted around the bike stalled in the middle of the road and flowed like a river on either side. And, inevitably, Ratan and Imran would always appear in the Sumo, waiting patiently for the bike to start or helping out if needed. Once the bikers realised this they relaxed a little and took their time thinking through the mechanics of the task.

By the first junction we'd lost sight of a good half of the group. We carried on and pulled up at the turn-off, conspicuously placing ourselves in the middle of the road to wave everyone down the correct route. We counted most of the group safely through, then Neil approached, closely followed by Owen. Neil was staring straight ahead and, despite our waving and gesticulations, he and Owen rode straight past within a metre of our bike, their white knuckles clenching the handgrips and grim gazes firmly focused on the road ahead.

I turned and looked at Lily, amazed.

'How could they not see us? Hang on. Here we go again!' We roared off in pursuit and caught up within a few hundred metres.

'Off on your own tour already!' I called. 'Try this way.'

We turned and were soon back on the Deeg road. A few minutes later we crossed the railway track to find half the group waiting under the shade of a mango tree, photographing a group of boys who had gathered to watch them.

'The others just rode on past like a bunch of lemmings,' said Karen. 'We tried to flag them down, but they didn't even see us.'

'Oh well. At least it's a fairly straight road from here. We should catch them up at the next village.'

The road to Deeg was two lanes of tarseal in fairly good condition and, in contrast to yesterday's drive from Delhi, carried fairly light traffic. These were the very reasons we'd chosen it for our first ride.

As we cruised the last stretch to Deeg I tucked in behind each of the group in turn, watching their riding style. Some were still stamping on the brake pedal when they wanted to change gear, forgetting that these controls were reversed on the Indian bikes. I knew this would soon pass as they got used to the Bullets. On the whole they were accomplished riders and looked quite comfortable and confident.

We caught up with the intrepid breakaway scouting party at the entrance to the town about 20 kilometres on. All the bikes had stopped, and everyone had crowded around one of them.

'Brian has a puncture, and Warren dropped his bike about ten kilometres back,' explained Alex. 'He's fine though, no problems there. And where's that railway crossing you told us about?' he asked.

'Oh, only about twenty kilometres back,' I replied. 'You rode right over it without seeing it? I'll point it out on the way back.'

Warren had had a minor spill while going through a village at low speed. He'd locked up the back wheel when avoiding a cow, but had only injured his dignity and bent a footrest. This was the first little accident of the tour, and I was a little uneasy that it had happened to the rider I felt the least confident about. But no real damage had been done. If this little spill was the worst that happened on the tour, we'd be happy.

Ratan and Imran pulled up behind the last of the stragglers. After a cursory glance at the bikes, and a slightly wounded glance at me, Imran opened the back of the Sumo, returning with a spare wheel and a couple of tools. He took to Warren's footrest with a hammer, straightening it with a couple of well-placed blows. The next job was to fix Brian's flat tyre.

'Stand back and give him some room,' I said, as Imran loosened the wheel nut on Brian's bike and yanked out the wheel spindle. I leaned the bike over on its side for him. Quick as a flash the old wheel was removed, and the new one put on and tightened up.

'Hell! That only took one and a half minutes!' marvelled Ken. 'Better than a racing pit stop!'

Imran grinned shyly and, as he gathered his tools together and returned them to the truck, he walked a little taller.

With the whole group united at least temporarily, we turned into the main street of Deeg. The road surface worsened immediately into a confusion of ruts, potholes and areas of ancient roadway loosely cobbled with boulders. On all sides, townspeople rushed from their doors to stand and stare at our deafening passage. We skirted the colossal turreted fort surrounded by a moat full of green evil-looking water, and drew up in the shade of the palace wall.

Just in front of us a low wall encircled the man-made lake bordering the palace. Even though the water in the lake, like that in the moat of the fort, was murky and rubbish-strewn, this didn't detract from the beauty of the palace whose frontage it bordered.

As we approached the main palace the guard stood up from his seat in the shade. I surreptitiously passed him a ten-rupee note as an encouragement to open the doors. Officially this area was closed to the public but, in a typically Indian way, with a little financial lubrication we were allowed to enter. My jitters about offering baksheesh had almost completely disappeared since that first nervous bribe in the Delhi train station. This time, the baksheesh included a guided tour of all the rooms of this fading glory.

The palace was built in the mid-1700s by the Maharaja Suraj Mahal, and was occupied as recently as the 1970s. Despite any sort of formal upkeep it was still an imposing building. The drawing room alone stretched 60 metres long and 30 metres wide, its ceilings soaring 10 metres above us. The room was crammed with enough ornate furniture and ornaments to make any antique dealer green with envy. The decaying settees and carpets gave an overwhelmingly ghostly 'Marie Celeste'-like feeling that this place had been suddenly and hastily deserted, its occupants not even taking the time to retrieve their splendid possessions.

We strolled through dusty rooms, eventually entering the vast formal dining room. At a mere 50 metres long this was slightly smaller than the drawing room, but was made grander by the 10-metre floor-to-ceiling arched windows overlooking the lake. A long table that would have seated close to a hundred diners dominated the room. With half-closed eyes we could imagine the extravagant dinner parties the maharajas once held for visiting dignitaries and officials.

Most of the maharajas, nawabs and nizams of India have fallen upon relatively hard times since 1947. Prior to this, under a series of individual treaties with the British, these royal families had ruled over more than five hundred princely states covering fully one-third of India's land and a quarter of her population, and had been empowered to raise their own taxes. This all came to an end at the time of India's independence, although until the early 1960s the maharajas continued to be paid privy purses by the government, proportional to their land holdings, to help maintain their fabulously wealthy lifestyles. Indira Ghandi put a stop to this system of propping up these redundant rulers, and they and their magnificent palaces and castles had since been left to their own devices. Many, if not most of them, had deserted their immense residences, unable to pay for their upkeep. The grand palaces were left to fall into ruin.

Some of the royals, who had seen the writing on the wall in the 1950s, had anticipated the tourist boom with remarkable prescience and converted parts of their palaces into upmarket hotels. Unfortunately for Deeg, and many other small places, most towns off the main tourist routes have no chance of being saved from the ravages of time. In Deeg's case the last maharaja died in 1967 and left no heir interested or wealthy enough to maintain the palace.

We left the crumbling palace and its ghosts and drifted into the formal gardens and their two thousand separate fountains laid out in a perfectly symmetrical pattern. Our watchman-cum-guide led us along the well-kept avenues and up a wide, twisting ramp that emerged on a high parapet overlooking the entire complex. Behind the parapet lay a swimming pool-sized reservoir with two pulley systems for drawing water up from the lake. Over thousands of hours of heaving buckets up to fill this reservoir, the ropes had carved deep furrows in the stone. A complicated series of valves and floodgates dominated one side of the pool. Our guide explained that it took two oxen teams working day and night a total of five days to fill the tank. Then, at the maharaja's command, the valves would be opened and the fountains would play for four hours.

The afternoon's shadows were lengthening so we gently hustled the group back to the bikes and began the start-up ritual again.

'Stay behind me for the trip home', I suggested to everyone who was listening and not gaping at some new distraction.

About 10 kilometres from Deeg we'd scheduled a chai stop in a small village. This was the first time that many of the group had experienced this unique Indian drink, and they crowded around watching the chai-wallah vigorously boiling tea, milk, cinnamon, crushed ginger, cardamom, sugar and several other spices in a saucepan over a kerosene stove. I ordered cups of chai for the entire group, not bothering to ask who wanted one, cajoling them with 'You've all got to try this at least once.'

'It's too hot for bloody tea!' grumbled Alex.

'Believe me, this is the most refreshing drink in India', I said. 'It's got a caffeine hit like a good espresso coffee. And it's safe to drink – it's all boiled.'

Everyone took one of the little earthenware cups of the sweet, strong, milky drink from the chai vendor's son. There were both grins and grimaces as the group tried this new taste experience.

'What do we do with the cups?' asked Warren, who'd drained his with relish.

'Just chuck them onto that pile of broken ones.' I waved at a pile of pottery fragments in the road next to the stand. 'They're disposable.'

Warren shook his head. As several locals threw their cups to the ground, shattering them, he quietly gathered up two or three intact ones and placed them carefully in his bag, much to the amusement of the crowd which had gathered to watch the show.

'I'll take these home as a souvenir,' he said. 'Though I think to these people that's a bit like someone going into a takeaway bar at home and keeping the milkshake cup!'

As we were finishing our drinks, a cacophony erupted from just beyond the crowd. Whilst we had been supping our chais a passing gypsy family had spotted us as a possible source of revenue, and had speedily set up their show on the roadside not 20 metres from the bikes. The mother and father sat beating a ferocious rhythm on their drums and cymbals and calling everyone within earshot to witness the marvels about to unfold. The crowd that had stood gawking at our group now deserted us for a far better spectacle. We hastily threw our chai cups away and edged between the onlookers, cameras at the ready.

The gypsy family had set up a couple of 4-metre-high poles supported by guy ropes. Between the poles a tightrope was stretched about 3 metres off the ground. A barefoot little girl, about six or seven years of age and clad in a heavily embroidered gypsy dress over ankle-length pantaloons, scampered up one of the poles. After we'd all quietened she stepped out onto the rope and walked along it, holding a horizontal balancing pole, as nonchalantly as if she were out for a stroll in the park.

This first, impressive traverse drew gasps of admiration from our group, but more was yet to come. When she turned around to recross the rope, she stopped in the middle. In perfect time to the drumming, she began to swing her feet and the rope from side to side, increasing the arc of the swing further and further. From the waist up her tiny body remained perfectly still, apart from slight twitches of the balancing pole, in what seemed like an impossible feat of balance. There was a sprinkling of applause from the crowd and the chink of a few coins in the plate passed around by one of her young brothers.

Then, to our astonishment, several brass water jugs were passed up to the girl. One by one she balanced them on her head, and then with expert control, she again started swinging her feet, the brass jugs suspended unmoving above her wildly oscillating legs. Just when her gyrations reached what seemed to be an unbeatable climax, she slowly lifted one foot from the rope, tucked it under her skirts, and continued to swing her other leg back and forth, balanced on one small foot.

Mouths dropped agape throughout the group at this extraordinary exploit, and as the plate was passed around again several notes appeared from the impressed bikies. As the show wound down, I saw the family counting up the contents of the plate. The mother spotted a fifty-rupee note – a small fortune to these people. She clasped her hands together and cast her gaze to the sky, thankful to the gods for sending these extravagant barbarians on bikes to her.

By the time we'd coaxed the group back along the road the sun had slipped toward the horizon, the light becoming softer and more photogenic by the minute. Women clad in rainbow-hued saris made irresistible pictures as they walked back home from their toil in the fields, or drew water from watering holes shared by bathing oxen. Before long the group was stretched out over several miles photographing everything that did and didn't move. Eventually, with Ratan and Imran's help we managed to chivvy them all along to our meeting point at the railway crossing, and then through the town in a fairly tight line to the hotel, just as the light suddenly failed.

We breathed a sigh of relief at having mustered everyone around the last corner and into the hotel garden before dark. Just then the last three bikes rode obliviously past the hotel entrance, heading towards Jaipur at a rate of knots.

'Order me a cold soda,' I called to Lily as I jumped back on the bike and raced off to retrieve the errant bikies.

'The cold beer's back this way!' I shouted as a couple of kilometres later I pulled alongside Neil, the foremost of the trio, who was by this time looking a bit puzzled at the lack of bikes in front of him.

When we finally herded everyone back, to my pleasant surprise Lalli and his wife Neelam and baby son Raunak had arrived at the hotel. For some time Lalli had been threatening to take a break from the office and join us on the road for a day or so.

'You look a bit hot and bothered, Steve,' remarked Neelam. 'No problems, I hope?'

'Oh no. Just the usual, a puncture, one minor accident and about twenty lost bikes,' I laughed. 'That's pretty good for the first ride.'

As we joined the group, who were all sitting in the garden, the excited buzz of laughter-filled conversation boded well for the trip ahead.

'We'll have no problems with this lot,' I said quietly to Lalli and Lily.

'So it would seem,' he said. 'I can't help remembering when I couldn't convince you that this was possible. Now look at you, king of the road!'

'Not without your help and bikes though!' I laughed, placing my arm around his shoulder, and calling for everyone's attention.

'I propose a toast,' I said, raising my glass. 'To Lalli's bikes, and a great first ride.'

Chapter Six

There was a sharp knock on the door.

'What the –!' I fumbled for the light switch in the darkness.

'It is five-forty-five sir. The safari leaves in twenty minutes,' came the timid response from beyond the door.

'It's definitely *your* turn, Daktari,' Lily insisted, pulling the sheets firmly over her head.

True enough, it was my turn. We'd agreed to take turns accompanying the clients on their dawn tiger safari at Ranthambhore National Park, so the other could get a bit of a lie-in. Somehow, over the last three tours, I'd found other compelling and urgent issues needing my personal attention at the hotel that prevented me from leaving my nice warm bed for the chilly drive. On this trip the ultimatum had been well and truly laid down by Lily. There was no way out.

I struggled into my warmest clothes and slipped out the door towards the restaurant, ignoring the low snicker from the bed. Even at this hour tea, coffee and biscuits had been laid out for us, and several of the early risers in the group were already cradling cups of steaming liquid. I sat on the steps next to Matt as he indulged in his newly acquired habit of smoking beedies, the ludicrously cheap and tiny cigarettes rolled in a tobacco leaf. In the distant darkness a mullah chanted the morning call to prayer from the mosque in town. Slowly the rest of the sleepy group congregated, and we chatted about the trip, the park and – most importantly to the group – the chances of seeing a tiger.

Ranthambhore National Park was once the hunting ground of the maharajas, and the current Duke of Edinburgh is said to have shot a large tiger in this very park. The area has been a wildlife sanctuary since the mid-1950s, and for the last thirty years has been one of nine parks set aside by India's Project Tiger programme as a 'safe haven' for tigers and other wildlife. The tiger population has increased slowly, despite suspicions that government employees have poached the tigers in the past to sell the most prized parts to the Chinese traditional medicine market. Just two weeks before our visit, the *Times of India* had reported that a truck carrying seven tiger skins and over fifty leopard skins had been stopped by police not one hundred kilometres from here.

Access to the park is strictly controlled with a system of government-run jeeps and cantors, or open-topped buses, running safaris on defined routes, morning and night. The best chances of seeing a tiger are late in the evening or very early in the morning. Hence our rude pre-dawn awakening.

The twenty-seat cantor we'd rented pulled up outside the hotel just as the faint red tinge of dawn appeared in the sky. The driver, guide and his friend introduced themselves as we climbed aboard. We'd barely got seated when the driver put his foot down and raced off along the narrow 8-kilometre road to the park gates.

'I thought biking here was scary, but this is bloody terrifying!' said Neil, clutching the edge of the seat in front of him.

I tried to signal the driver to slow down a little, but he turned to me, completely disregarding the road. 'We must be getting to the park early for good chance of tiger spotting, sahib.'

He turned his eyes back to the road just in time to swerve from the path of an unlit camel cart. Not surprisingly, we were the first cantor to the gates. As the guide handed over our tickets at the park office, the driver smiled at the still-quivering group. 'You see, we are first. There will be no other cantors scaring off the tigers now.'

As we drove through the gates, I explained to everyone that it was traditional to give a generous tip if we were fortunate enough to spot a tiger.

'At least the driver's trying hard!' said Jeanine. 'Let's hope we get there alive, though.'

In the chill dawn a pink glow spread down the cliff tops and across the savannah lands of the sanctuary. Apart from the creaks of our cantor grunting along the gravel track, it was so quiet and calm we could almost forget this was India. A pair of spotted chital deer nibbled leaves from dhok trees with complete disregard for the many pairs of eyes turned on them and, apparently, without fear of tiger attack.

This didn't seem a hopeful sign. While we didn't necessarily want to see the graceful chital savaged in front of our eyes, there was a mild expectation in the group that they would spot at least one of the twenty-odd tigers in the park. I'd been clear about our chances – twenty percent or less – but it was still early, and hopes were reasonably high.

'There are some deer that have never seen a tiger,' I remarked. A groan from the entire group reminded me that, sometimes, weak humour is inappropriate in a tour guide.

As we pushed deeper into the park, chital and the larger sambar deer became more common and appeared less nervous. A few nilgai antelope stared at us from behind trees. In a nearly dry watering hole an obese crocodile basked in the morning sun.

'This drought is good for crocodiles,' said the guide. 'Plenty of food for them and easy to catch as the water gets lower.'

An hour and a half into the safari, we had reached the turn-around point of our journey. We'd seen monkeys, a mongoose and wild boar, but no tiger. A resigned feeling settled over both guides and bikies. Not much chance of a tiger now, I thought. Best to get them back for breakfast as quickly as possible.

Just then the guide signalled to the driver to pull over. He turned to us with his finger to his lips.

'Shhh!' he hissed. 'I just heard the alarm call of the wood crow. There could be a tiger over there.'

He pointed down a rough and narrow track winding down a dry riverbed.

'Let's go then,' I whispered.

'This is not an official track and it is forbidden to go here sir. Just wait.'

He stood up high on the windscreen of the cantor, tense and listening for several minutes. Some of the group shifted restlessly, yawning and sighing. An air of cynicism became plain as the minutes dragged on. A faint bird call sounded every so often. More minutes went by. Finally, the guide and driver held a hushed conference.

'We will go off the official track now. Please maintain absolute silence.'

The cantor was slowly eased down the riverbed track, which fell away quite precipitously to our left and deteriorated into a couple of vague ruts in the grass.

'If we are caught here by the game guards we will be in big trouble, so silence please,' repeated the guide.

We crept along for another hundred metres, with everyone holding their breath.

'Yess!' hissed the guide. The cantor stopped sharply. 'Over there, on the other side of the river!' He pointed into the long grass.

The entire group surged to one side of the cantor and peered eagerly into the scrub.

'Where? Where's the tiger?'

Suddenly, we could see the almost perfectly camouflaged feline, prone in the grass less than twenty-five metres from us. How the sharp-eyed guide had spotted the tiger was a mystery. The animal's bold stripes helped it to blend to near invisibility against the waving yellow grass. I reached down to get my video camera and when I brought it up to shoot the scene, I spent some anxious moments trying to find the tiger again. Through the telephoto lens I could see blood on the tiger's snout and peacock feathers strewn all around, the remains of a nice little breakfast snack.

The bikers' cameras clicked away furiously. The guide and driver were as happy as cats with two tails, their tip assured now. The tiger lay almost completely still, gazing directly at us in a bored, faintly hostile way. After a few minutes it yawned, stood up, stretched, then turned its back to us and lay down again. Obviously, we weren't nearly as fascinating to the tiger as it was to us.

'We must get going now,' urged the guide. 'We are going to be late and the game guards will cause us trouble.'

The cantor backed up the riverbed to the road, and we were

treated to another high-speed adventure ride through the park so that we could reach the gate before the nine-thirty closing time. Just before the gates we stopped for a moment and the third man, who had been quietly seated in the front throughout the safari, dismounted and walked off down a sidetrack.

'Who was he?' I asked the guide, puzzled.

'Oh, he's a game guard. He is just going off on patrol. Don't worry. He is our friend and won't report us.'

I shook my head. India never failed to surprise me.

As we drove back to the hotel the excited group had a whip-round, and our successful guiding duo received a substantial tip when they dropped us off. I headed straight for our room to throw Lily out of bed and take her place for an hour or two of much-needed sleep.

When I awoke a couple of hours later, most of the group had gone off in search of souvenirs. The urge to spend rupees on just about everything from tiger t-shirts to toe rings was good for the merchants of the nearby town of Sawai Madhopur, but even this early in the trip the baggage was beginning to take on ominous proportions. Every day Ratan had to wrestle with yet more bags crammed with silk saris, shoes, silver jewellery, wall hangings, carved stone turtles and elephants, cushions, and even the tasselled tinsel that decorated every Tata truck. Luckily, having the luggage strapped on the Sumo's roof rack meant that the shopping could go on pretty much unchecked.

Later in the evening the brothers Neil and Brian swaggered into the hotel courtyard sporting their newest purchases – waistcoats luridly embroidered with red, green and yellow elephants. We admired their outfits while being grateful they hadn't bought the matching hats. Since they were all dressed up in such fine attire, we decided to go for dinner outside our hotel. Lily and I knew just the place.

Despite its somewhat seedy appearance the Sharma Hotel was one of the best vegetarian restaurants in town. The dirt-besmirched walls and swipes at our plates by a waiter wielding a damp and dubious rag belied the fine cuisine whipped up by the cook under conditions that would have most Western 'chefs' throwing temper tantrums. Using the single charcoal-fired stove and tandoori oven which took up street space outside the restaurant – the better to cram more customers inside – the cook turned out cashew nut curries, roasted eggplants, garlic and tomato puree, fried lady's fingers, birianis, paneer cheese curries and the most perfect rotis.

The roti-making was a performance in itself. First the tandoori man flattened small round balls of dough into perfect discs merely by tossing them from hand to hand. He then deftly reached deep into the fiercely hot oven with his bare hand and stuck the discs of dough against the oven wall. The rotis puffed up and bubbled merrily on the oven wall for a minute or two before being flicked onto the coals for a last few seconds' crisping. This was not a trick to be tried by the untutored, and this veteran had obviously spent a great part of his life in front of the tandoori oven.

Stacks of fresh rotis and plates of mouth-watering food just kept coming. By this stage of the tour Owen had wised up to the amount of chilli lurking in some of these meals, and he'd come prepared. By draping a small hand-towel around his neck, he was free to sweat in quite impressive rivers without having to stop eating for any inconvenient face-mopping. The 'towel scale' became the new way to rate the 'chilli factor' in our meals. Medium hot was a 'one-towel' meal, hot was 'two towels'. Most of our meals were 'one-towel', which was a good thing as Owen only ever brought along one towel.

Emboldened by his jaunty waistcoat and a few Kingfisher beers, Neil filched one of Matt's beedies after the last grains of biriani had been eaten and parked himself in the cashier's seat. I was relieved that he'd decided to steal the cashier's job instead of trying his hand at roti-making.

'Five hundred rupees each', he demanded, puffing away furiously.

This absurd price – meals for all of us cost the grand sum of 600 rupees – prompted jeers and cries of 'Get off, ya wally' from the group and laughs from the restaurant staff, who nevertheless looked a little hopeful.

'Chuck them out', Neil continued, waving a dismissive hand at the rest of our group, to the great amusement of the Sharma Hotel's owner, Mr Sharma. 'They're a bunch of troublemakers, these Kiwis.'

When the cashier finally managed to evict him from his seat and collect our bill, another 'treat' was in store for us. One of the best paan makers in the town was just around the corner, promised Mr Sharma. He led the way down one of the dark and dung-spattered lanes near the restaurant. Standing amongst the rubbish we gathered round the paan-wallah as he made the Indian version of an after-dinner mint. He methodically filled bright green paan leaves with lime paste, betel nut pieces, cardamom and several different chutneys. He then rolled the whole concoction into tight green packets. We each took one of these rather large paan and stuffed them into our cheeks. The waistcoat brigade got the first chew. They were still chewing long after some of the others had explosively spat theirs out amongst the rest of the rubbish.

Mr Sharma, though, was so charmed by the group's dining and

paan-chewing habits that he insisted we return to the restaurant the next day for a farewell chai. It seemed rude to refuse, even though I was a little impatient to get a good start in the morning for our ride on what was a tricky part of the journey. The group decided to try to walk off their enormous meals, so Lily and I rode back with Ratan in the Sumo.

On the lightless drive back from the Sharma Hotel, a small disaster struck. The Sumo collided with a stack of unmarked pipes sticking off the back of a parked tractor invisible in the dark. One of the pipes hit the windscreen with a mighty thump and then slid under the roof rack, ripping it clean off the Sumo and flinging it onto the road. Ratan, although much rattled by the collision, collected himself and scrambled out of the Sumo to pick up the remains of the rack.

But it was too late. By the time he reached the spot where the rack should have been, it was gone. Some opportunistic villagers had sneaked up, seized the rack and hidden it in the neighbouring fields. Our ballooning baggage situation had just become critical.

Negotiations commenced, rivalling a 'Camp David peace summit' in their length and complexity. Much was made of the price of the rack and potential damage to the pipes and tractor, which the villagers considered to be the innocent victims in this drama. The idea that someone from Delhi, the source of all wealth in their minds, could come along and litter the road with their roof rack was an affront to these 'simple, honest' folk. That we would think twice about paying a king's ransom for the rack was equally ludicrous.

The mortified hotel manager spent a fruitless hour trying to broker a deal. Mr Sharma also went in to bat on our behalf and came back shrugging his shoulders. The bottom line was that, if we wanted the remains of the roof rack back, we would have to pay 4000 rupees. Even threats of police action did nothing to reduce the ransom. I began to suspect that there were police connections amongst the villagers.

Ratan was stressed almost to the point of tears, having lost a great deal of face by getting us into this situation.

I tried to cheer him up. 'We can purchase another rack tomorrow in the market,' I said. 'How much does a new rack cost?'

'In Delhi it is only costing eight hundred rupees,' was the reassuring reply.

Eight hundred rupees was a whole lot less than 4000 rupees, by anyone's maths. We decided to stop negotiations and let the villagers keep their ill-gotten prize.

When we finally arrived back at the hotel most of the group was sprawled around tables in the gardens sipping nightcaps, unaware of the roof-rack kidnapping. I told them the story.

'Four thousand rupees or the roof rack dies,' I recounted gleefully. Away from the tension of the negotiations, it all seemed rather funny.

My sense of humour faded with every passing minute the next morning as we scoured the hardware shops and bazaars of the bustling town. Not a roof rack for a Sumo was to be had at any price. Was I getting paranoid or was the whole town involved in the conspiracy?

'These village people are very low class,' sniffed Ratan, demonstrating the mutual distrust that exists between Delhi-ites and just about anyone else in India. 'Perhaps in Bundi is possible purchasing roof rack,' he suggested hopefully.

'Will we get all the luggage inside the Sumo?' I asked, equally hopeful.

'Oh, no problem sir,' he replied. 'Is possible fitting many more luggages.'

Buoyed by Ratan's optimism we decided to defer the roof-rack purchase problem until Bundi, our next stop.

Sure enough, the next morning came and to my relief all the bags, boxes and bike parts were somehow squeezed into the vehicle with space to spare. Still, I didn't fancy the chances of fitting an unwell biker or two on top of it all. But we couldn't toss out any of the spare parts – they were essential in case of breakdowns – and I was sure that none of the group would be keen to part with their shopping.

As we gathered everyone together and asked the interminable 'Have you got all your stuff?' questions, I remembered our invitation of last night from Mr Sharma. The thought of getting us all through the chaotic traffic in town to his restaurant, parked and then back through town onto the main road to Bundi was a bit daunting at this early hour.

'Perhaps we'll just leave the chai invite for another time,' I said to Lily, who speedily agreed. 'He probably won't be there anyway.'

Everyone started their bikes and we set off on the next leg of our journey. But any hopes we had of sneaking out of town unnoticed – as if a whole group of Westerners on motorcycles *could* sneak out of town – were dashed as we turned left out of the hotel gate. Waiting 100 metres down the road was Mr Sharma, astride his own Bullet.

'There goes *that* plan,' I muttered to Lily as we reluctantly fell in behind our now extremely happy guide. His obvious pride and joy at leading his own gang of Western bikers through the town quickly dispelled any irritation I had felt at having to delay our departure.

Our arrival at the restaurant caused quite a stir. The crowd of mostly men and boys pushing in all around made parking in a row, as Mr Sharma requested, impossible. Mr Sharma rushed around demanding chai from his still bleary-eyed staff and trying his best to organise a photograph of us all. We drank our chai and stood bemused at the centre of an inquisitive crowd who had stopped to see what the fuss was about. As the dozens of eyes stared at us, I knew what that tiger must have felt like.

One of the restaurant workers brought fresh golden garlands of marigolds and frangipani that Mr Sharma draped over each of our heads.

'These flowers are to bless you on the next part of your journey,' he said. 'It is a difficult road to Bundi, but you will be safe now.'

I gave some thought to his words. Time for another safety talk soon, I decided. They're getting a bit overconfident.

As we edged our bikes through the throng Mr Sharma insisted on escorting us out of town and onto the Bundi road. I'm sure that if we'd asked him, he would have dropped everything and led us all the way to Pakistan.

Chapter Seven

The narrow road to Bundi twisted through many small villages of mud-plastered huts decorated with white traditional symbols. Out in the fields, women in brightly coloured saris shaped fresh cow dung into neat patties, to be dried and used later for fuel.

A chirping like flocks of birds grew louder as we passed through one village, but then we realised it wasn't the sound of birds at all. The roar of our Bullets had brought blue-uniformed schoolchildren of all sizes racing out of the school. All of the children lined up cheering and waving at us from the side of the road, or ran alongside trying to keep up. It was hard not to feel like royalty, and hard not to feel quite humbled. Time and time again this scene played out in many Rajasthani villages, most of which seemed to harbour an endless supply of cheerful blue-clad children.

At our next chai stop a crowd of villagers appeared from nowhere as we settled around the astonished chai maker and his wife. With the group more or less captive in one place, it seemed a good opportunity for my safety talk.

'You're all riding really well,' I said, 'but this is probably the most dangerous part of the journey. You may be feeling on top of the situation and having a good time, but don't get cocky. This *is* India and there are heaps of maniacs and potholes out there, waiting to get you.'

The casual acknowledgements and relaxed smiles all around gave me the feeling that everyone was coping just fine and that they didn't need any lectures from 'Captain Chapati', thank you very much.

We headed out on the final leg of about 80 kilometres to Bundi, through what most Indian city-dwellers would call 'bandit country'.

ᏮᏗ

Lily and I had travelled this particular stretch many times. On our first nervous ride here four years ago, we'd spent a fantastic few days in Bundi and had been eager to ride to Ranthambhore to see the famed tigers. The monsoon season had not really ended, but we had no raingear or anything else needed to ride in wet weather. The road followed along a steep escarpment to our left and, up ahead in the distance, ominous black rain clouds were tumbling off the cliffs towards the road.

About 30 kilometres outside Bundi, all hell broke loose. Torrential rain, hail and wind tore into us. Through the rapidly diminishing visibility a small thatched hutch appeared and, as we drew closer, a couple of brightly turbaned, moustachioed goatherds beckoned. Given the rain and hail drilling down on our heads we had no choice but to comply and take our chances that these weren't the dreaded 'bandits' we'd been warned about. We stooped down and hurried into the low-roofed dwelling. Inside were seven other shelter-seekers, and a number of smelly goats.

Space was quickly made for us in the driest part of the hut, though this was pretty wet by most standards as the poorly thatched roof was rapidly becoming waterlogged and leaking. No one spoke a word of English, so we crouched down smiling and laughing at the madness of the weather and at their terrified goats trying to push into the hut. Brown streams appeared around the hut and quickly grew into small rivers, and we all found stones to perch on to keep our feet 'dry'.

More and more goatherds sought shelter in the hut as the rain poured down. Although it became crowded in the extreme and I was scrunched up with them all, it was as though a force field existed about a foot all around Lily. They were all friendly enough to her, but not one of them would venture near her. This, we found later, was normal respectful behaviour. For a man to touch another man's wife, even accidentally, would be considered a tremendous insult by these folk. In the crowded conditions of the hut this was a courtesy beyond belief.

As suddenly as the storm began, it stopped. All of the goatherds disappeared from the hut just as suddenly, leaving us standing like a couple of drowned rats in the waterlogged landscape.

৩৯

But this time, on our seventh tour, the weather couldn't have been more different. It was perfect, sunny and hot, and the road dry. It was an excellent day for the ride to Bundi.

During our chai stops, talking to the men in the villages was easy. The crowds that gathered when we stopped along the way were exclusively male, and many of the men and boys spoke enough English to talk about cricket, if nothing else. But true to Hindu tradition it was virtually impossible for us strangers, male or female, to approach the Indian village women in these rural areas.

Iridescent in their beautiful saris and veils they hung back in groups, half-hidden in the shadows. But all along the roads they could always be seen walking along in graceful lines, carrying the most bizarre and unlikely loads on their heads. Bricks, hay bales, suitcases and even a small engine would go by perfectly balanced. We all had nothing but admiration for these slightly built women who toted their burdens seemingly with ease. Most of the group was uncomfortably aware that the women in these poor areas replaced the beasts of burden their families couldn't afford.

We edged through the narrow lanes of one of the larger villages and once again it became a challenge to thread our way around the crowds. Despite his best attempts to keep his bike under control, Neil's front wheel grazed a slow-moving pedestrian. The man jumped as though he'd been shot, but luckily he was unhurt. It was a caution to us all to pay attention in these congested conditions.

As we approached yet another railway crossing, the inevitable happened. Warning lights flashed, bells sounded and the barrier arms creaked slowly down. A few mad devils on scooters dashed underneath, risking decapitation or at least a good knock on their heads. But we accepted this latest delay on our journey with a sort of fatalism. Turning off the bikes' engines we settled down to wait. Ahead of us were about a dozen Tata trucks, some Ambassador cars, and many other thwarted motorcyclists.

No sooner had the barrier come down than a couple of hawkers appeared.

'Chai! Chai!' one of them called out. He strolled down the queue, deftly balancing atop his turban a large brass tray with a clay charcoal burner heating his jug of chai, which was circled by clay cups.

Since there was nothing else to do, we beckoned him over. He unfolded a small wire stand, placed the tray on it and poured out the chai orders into the rough cups.

As we twiddled our thumbs and drank our chai another truck

pulled up to the barrier. But this one stopped in the wrong lane, completely blocking the way for the vehicles on the other side of the road. Not wanting to be left out, a few more crowded in, then a few more. Soon a tangle of carts, trucks and cars blocked both lanes on either side of the crossing. It seemed impossible that this snarl would sort itself out, but no one seemed the slightest bit perturbed.

Five minutes ticked away. There was still no sign of any train. We peered into the distance, searching for the cause of our hold-up. Still no train. I couldn't help thinking how lucky the chai-wallah was to have such a captive market for his tea.

Luck, as it turned out, had nothing to do with it. As soon as the chai-wallah had emptied his jug and made himself a few rupees richer, he gave an almost imperceptible nod to the barrier operator, who disappeared back into the booth. We sat back on our bikes, prepared to wait yet another eternity.

But only a few seconds later the barrier arms swung up. Lily and I looked at each other, flabbergasted. We'd waited at the railway crossing for the exact length of time needed to sell a pot of chai. This was definitely commerce, not karma.

None of the locals was even slightly put out by the fact that no train ever came. With horns blaring and indignant gesticulations, the other drivers were all too busy jockeying and pushing for the best and fastest position to get across the tracks that they themselves had blocked. The several trucks hogging the wrong side of the road on both sides of the tracks had caused a massive traffic jam, which entertained us hugely while we pulled on our helmets and other gear. Several minutes later we threaded our way through the pande-monium, which had rapidly degenerated into a fierce argument between two truckies stopped firmly on the train tracks, each insisting loudly and repeatedly that the other give way.

Finally back on the open road, the sun beat down without relief. It was the hottest day of the ride so far. Along the way there were plenty of opportunities to stop for photos of villagers going about their daily tasks, for drinks of water and to reload yet more film in the cameras. This was the most snap-happy group we'd had to date, and not one watering hole or passing camel went unphotographed. Alex spent much of his time with one eye clamped to his video camera's viewfinder, bellowing out a hearty travelogue for the benefit of the folks back home.

To be fair, the sights of Rajasthan are among the most colourful any traveller could find anywhere, and it would have been ridiculous not to stop. Herds of camels resting under a grove of mango trees caused much excitement, until we came upon a scattering of women gathered at a river beating the day's laundry clean on large flat rocks. This fascinated the photographers for a short while, until someone noticed a lotus-covered lake on the other side of the road. Not only was a lake something of a novelty in this dry region, but the sight of a man and a boy piloting a small punt through the lake, collecting the lotus roots, had many shutters clicking. Later, we passed roadside vendors roasting the knobbly round roots to black, unappealing lumps on charcoal braziers.

At one particularly photogenic scene Karen and Ken pulled up beside some of the other bikies. Although the heat was stifling, these two, who'd been nicknamed 'the careful Canucks', always wore long trousers, long-sleeved jackets and full-faced helmets.

KAREN GOA

Above

The 'careful Canuks', Ken and Karen, ready to ride in Bundi.

Right

Ken and Karen's Bullet, crumpled in a ditch near Bundi. The locals were quick to arrive on the scene to help with the rescue.

KEN GOA

Always look out for cows – one of India's usual road hazards!

Village women do an impressive balancing act, near Deeg.

KAREN GOA

Painted oxen are one way to get around...

...or you can try a camel.

KAREN GOA

Left

This 'baori' (stepwell) in Bundi was constructed in 1699.

Below

Colourful vegetables are heaped up at a market in Bundi.

Right

A sacred cow has a bit of a nosey in a Bundi house.

Below

For sale: marigolds and roses for puja garlands at the Bundi market.

OWEN HASKELL

OWEN HASKELL

This milkman is on his way to town.

Milk market in Bundi.

Giggling beggar girls take time out to watch magic tricks, New Delhi.

The road that wasn't – on the outskirts of Bundi.

JENNY COOPER

Left
Rao Singh, Hotel Bijaipur Castle.

Below
The Indian Motorcycle Adventurers, Hotel Bijaipur Castle.

STEVE KRZYSTYNIAK

'Aren't you hot?' asked some of the less cautious sorts, cool and comfortable in their short-sleeved shirts and shorts.

'It's only hot when we stop riding,' panted Karen, sweat dripping off her nose. 'I'm not really keen on riding in short sleeves, with all these scary Tata truck drivers and dozy cows on the road.' There were a few muffled snorts over this overweening caution, but the Canadians' helmets and jackets stayed on.

The last section of the road to Bundi was more or less straight and free from the potholes we'd come to expect. I could tell the group was itching to have a bit of a go on this stretch.

'Let's meet up again in about twenty kilometres, but be careful –'

I'd barely got the words out of my mouth before the group zoomed off down the road.

Lily and I fell back a little behind the group. We had a social call to make.

&

On the previous tour, Lily and I had stopped by a particularly photogenic traditional Rajasthani farmhouse standing alone a short distance from the road. It was a beautifully proportioned one-room dwelling with walls of reddish-brown earth, decorated with stylised mandana paintings of peacocks, lotus flowers and camels in white paint. Within minutes we were surrounded by the entire curious family.

Canadian Dave, a burly vet from a small Alberta town, stopped when he saw our bikes. Then the Sumo pulled up and Ratan and Imran got out to see what the excitement was. We rummaged in our supplies and found biscuits to give to the eight or so thin children crowding around.

'These people very poor,' said Ratan, as he pulled out some bananas and oranges from the Sumo. 'No crops this year, drought causing.'

As the children ravenously devoured all the fruit and biscuits we offered them their mother, a careworn woman barely in her thirties, smiled weakly at us. Her right arm stuck out at an awkward angle and was covered with makeshift plaster. It had been badly broken. Lily examined the rough bandage with professional concern.

'Her arm is healing very badly. It needs resetting – it should be fine after that,' she said. 'But if it's left like this I think she'll have very limited movement.'

'Tell her she should see a doctor,' I urged Ratan. He spoke to the woman, and after a few minutes' discussion he translated, 'These people not having money for a doctor.'

'How much will the doctor cost?' I asked.

There was another exchange, and then came the answer. 'Maybe one hundred rupees.'

A hundred rupees! Five New Zealand dollars was all that stood between this woman, whose livelihood depended on hard physical work, and a healthy arm.

I got an assurance via Ratan that she would go immediately to the doctor. Then I handed her the hundred-rupee note. We gathered up all the snacks we had in the Sumo and gave them to the children. Dave pressed another hundred rupees into her hand, gesturing that this was to buy more food. As we mounted up and rode off, I was sure that I saw a tear in the eye of this tough Canadian – they certainly weren't far from mine.

☙

Lily and I were determined to call on the family again on our next tour, and we had vowed to return. Two months later here we were, making our promised visit. The family had been alerted by the other bikes passing, and were waiting at the roadside for us. As we dismounted the woman held her arm out, smiling, to Lily. She twisted it and flexed her wrist to show off the healed limb.

Calling Ratan over to translate, she told us that she had prayed for our safe return every day since we'd left. Seeing her happy and healed was worth many, many hundreds of rupees. We gave her a handful of photographs that Dave had taken, which would likely be the only images they'd ever have of their children. As we headed off to catch up with the current group I thought over and over about how, for the price of a couple of cappuccinos, we'd had the opportunity to change someone's life for the better.

A little while later we pulled up at the meeting place we'd arranged with the group, a shady spot 30 kilometres from Bundi at the junction with the Kota road. The fastest riders had already arrived. In the next few minutes most of the group trickled in.

As we waited for Alex, Ken and Karen, the last stragglers, a few minutes stretched into ten, then fifteen. An uneasy feeling crept into the pit of my stomach. Finally, Alex rolled up.

'I got a puncture,' he explained.

That was a relief. Punctures were a minor event, and Imran always dealt with these quickly.

'Ken and Karen were just behind me. They should be here any minute.'

We stared into the distance, waiting for them to come into view. Another few minutes crawled by. Finally Alex muttered, 'They should be here by now. I'm going to find them,' and headed back down the road.

Not two minutes later, Alex roared up beside us.

'Ken and Karen have dropped their bike into a ditch!'

My worst fears had come true. The safety talk obviously hadn't worked as well as I'd hoped. I jumped on my bike and roared back to the accident scene, hoping for the best.

But as I rounded the first bend my heart nearly stopped. Their bike lay on its tail amidst the yellow and orange litter of smashed tail-lights, at the bottom of a two-metre deep, rock-lined ditch. Ken was slumped on the roadside looking decidedly shaken, while Karen stood nearby, fuming and fiddling with her brand-new, now-broken camera. This looked hopeful – at least they weren't lying crumpled on the road. I jumped off the bike.

'Are you alright?' I asked them both, trying to calm my racing heart. 'What happened?'

After a few deep breaths, Karen told me the story. Several of the riders, including Ken, had been seduced by the straightway and had pushed their machines to the limit. As Ken rounded one of the few bends on this stretch he hit a bit of loose gravel, and the bike slid sideways. It shot off the road, skidded into the ditch and fell over onto its left side, tossing them off at the bottom like rag dolls in a cloud of dust.

Despite this spectacular dismount, they both looked and sounded a lot healthier than they should have been after a high-speed tumble into a gully. No bones were broken. A trickle of blood leaked out from under Karen's trouser leg where her shin had hit a rock. Deep scratches ran across her face visor. Ken's hip and elbow were grazed, and his leather jacket was ripped along one sleeve. Luckily, the 170-kilogram bike with its red-hot muffler hadn't landed on top of them.

A truckload of locals had just pulled up and were beginning to dismount to form a noisy, excited crowd. A moment later the Sumo with Imran, Ratan and the first-aid kit appeared round the corner. Yet again Imran gave me that slightly wounded look as he investigated the wreck. Some of the crowd helped us pull the bike up onto the road, whilst the rest of them milled about, offering advice and getting in the way.

Looking at the deep, rocky ditch and the two shaken but mostly uninjured riders, Ratan murmured, 'Maybe that woman's prayers working for you. They very lucky.'

Maybe her prayers had worked. Or maybe it was Mr Sharma's good luck garlands. We'd never know.

Once the bike had been hauled from the ditch, Imran checked it over thoroughly. It had suffered a lot more damage than its passengers. Broken exhaust pipe, rear mudguard, footrests, lights, luggage carrier, and brake pedal. It looked a mess.

'Twenty minutes is fixing,' he pronounced, making a beeline for the tools and spares in the back of the Sumo. It was a good thing that, even with the roof rack gone, there was still plenty of room for all the spare bike parts.

My efforts to help were just making Imran nervous, so we left him to conjure up a rideable Bullet out of this battered wreck in a mere twenty minutes, and all rode and limped back to the junction. As we waited, Lily cleaned and patched up the couple's few minor grazes.

'That one could have been nasty without a jacket,' said Owen – another one who'd been riding in his shirtsleeves – as Lily cleaned Ken's skinned elbow. The cautious nature of the 'careful Canucks' had paid off that day.

As I tried to slow my heart rate down, I thought about the near disaster. No lecture needed here, I thought. But I couldn't help myself.

'I think we've all learned something from that,' I said.

There were no dissenting voices to *this* wisdom from 'Captain Chapati'.

Imran was as good as his word. Almost exactly twenty minutes later we heard the grunt of the damaged bike through the bushes as Imran rode it into view. The bike looked dusty and scuffed up but miraculously was running well.

'Myself riding broken bike to Bundi for steering checking,' Imran said with a sheepish grin. The 'steering checking' gave Imran, a keen biker, a good excuse to get out of the Sumo and onto the Bullet.

Even though I thought that neither of them was in a state to drive I was anxious to get the Canadians back on the bikes as soon as possible, to avoid any 'falling off a horse' syndrome. But, although the accident left the bike worse for wear, it hadn't dented its riders' enthusiasm for motorcycling. Lily joined Ratan in the Sumo, Ken climbed on behind Alex, and Karen sat pillion on the back of my bike. She was obviously unnerved by the crash and felt stiff and tense behind me. But after a few minutes, and no further incidents, she relaxed enough to lean back and enjoy the view.

The accident slowed down the daredevils in the group to a less breakneck speed. It was a much more thoughtful bunch that carried on for the last few kilometres into Bundi, as each rider contemplated what *could* have happened after crashing into a two-metre gully at 70 kilometres per hour. Over the next couple of days, a few more helmets appeared on a few more heads.

Chapter Eight

No other traffic hazards, apart from the normal Indian ones, came our way on the remainder of the ride into Bundi. We rode into town in a loose line, a distant view of the fort and palace towering above the city giving a foretaste of the secrets of this ancient place.

Approaching the last roundabout just outside our hotel, the Ishwari Niwas, I decided to take a short-cut on the wrong side of the roundabout, to zip more quickly into the hotel entrance just on the other side. Most roundabouts in India are jammed with traffic going in all directions at once, and there's never a traffic cop in sight to make any sense of the situation. In typically perverse Indian style this one had absolutely no traffic but did have a very alert traffic cop who bossily directed us, via vigorous blasts on his whistle, to stop that Westernised traffic nonsense immediately and go around the proper way. Slightly chastened, we did, and we all pulled up with a roar of engines to the entrance of the hotel, whose sign promised 'A Royal Luxurious Comfort'.

Bundi is a small, bustling and endlessly fascinating city, but it's well off the main Rajasthani tourist circuit and has only a few places to stay. Over the years we'd tried most of them, with wildly differing degrees of success.

෴

When reconnoitring in preparation for our first-ever tour we'd taken the advice of a guidebook and approached the Haveli guest-house at the top of town. As we entered the tranquil courtyard of this 300-year-old building we struck up a conversation with a young couple sitting in one of the shady corners. They told us they were paying the reasonable sum of 350 rupees per night for one of the best rooms. They also let slip that they thought the 'old man' who owned the hotel was 'a bit creepy'.

Not ones to be frightened off by creepy old men we searched out the owner's son Mukash, and presented our proposal of bringing regular groups of ten or more bike riders to their property. In other guesthouses throughout Rajasthan we'd negotiated a substantial discount from the normal 'walk-in' room rates for our groups, and we opened discussions on this basis.

Not so, according to the father who had just emerged from the kitchen. To his way of thinking, and by some strange logic, group rates should be much higher than for individuals. He started the bartering process at a whopping 1200 rupees per room.

After bargaining long and hard we eventually settled on 500 rupees per room, much to the apparent disgust of both men. Mukash wrote out a detailed receipt for our deposit, listing all the room numbers. We went on our way, fairly – although not entirely – confident that all would be well.

Months later when we returned with our first group, Mukash and his father placed welcoming garlands over each of our clients' heads. Everything appeared to be fine, and it seemed that our previous misgivings were a bit paranoid.

But when Lily started to allocate the rooms to our clients, most were not the fairly spacious ones we'd been shown previously. Instead, these rooms were much smaller, pokier places, some barely bigger than the bed. We were quick to challenge the owners about this. But our misgivings turned out to be justified after all. These two were well prepared, and our protests got us nowhere. With a sinking feeling I remembered that we hadn't noted the actual numbers of the rooms we'd been shown on our former visit, trusting that the pair would surely not be *that* devious. The two conspirators led us around the rooms, ticking each number off against the list on our receipt.

'You see. It is all as we agreed,' said the father, triumphantly tapping the paper. This was certainly not how we saw it. For now, though, there was nothing to be done unless we wanted to treat the clients to a stand-up row.

'You know that this is *not* what we agreed,' I snapped, and we retreated to our room before things could get messy.

Our room, or our 'cell', as we'd begun to call it, was a tiny alcove off the dining room. A warped hardboard partition with a large gap, top and bottom, separated the two. The bed took up all the space in the room, and Lily and I both had to climb onto it to make space to close the door. A toilet in the corner lacked plumbing completely, but a bucket of dubious-looking water was provided for our 'convenience' for flushing the loo. The grubby concrete floor tilted from one side to the other by a slope of around six inches, and bricks had been shoved under the legs on one side of the bed in a failed attempt to level it. Every time one of us moved suddenly, one of the legs would fall off its brick with a crash, tipping us into the wall. This was definitely not the experience we had envisioned for our clients in Bundi, our favourite town in Rajasthan.

During the afternoon several of our clients came to us dismayed at the lack of hot water in their rooms after their long and dusty ride. Each time we attempted to sort this out the father tersely demanded 'Which room wants hot water *now*?' as outraged as if we'd clamoured for gilt-plated showerheads. Then he'd stride to a cupboard in the kitchen hiding a huge bank of frighteningly ancient switches, all presumably linked to the hot-water heaters, and begrudgingly switch one on. Fifteen minutes later he'd return and flick the power to that room off again. This ridiculous situation became something of a nightmare as more sweaty bikers demanded hot showers. We spent a most frustrating afternoon chasing him around from hot-water cupboard to room.

The day deteriorated further when one of our clients emerged from her room with a cup of tea she'd made with her nifty little travelling immersion heater. We'd all admired this gadget and had borrowed it on occasion to boil a cup of water. As she sat down in the garden with her tea that had obviously not come from the kitchens the old man completely lost his head, screaming that she should not be 'stealing' electricity by cooking in her room. He promptly scurried off to his switchboard and turned off the electricity for all our rooms. It took another set of lengthy negotiations with Mukash to restore the power. By this time, we'd had enough of these mean hosts.

'We'll just have to drop Bundi out of the next trip. Or maybe we can stay in Kota and do a day trip here,' said Lily rather wistfully, back in our alcove. 'It's a pity there's no other hotel in town big enough.'

The decision made to dump the Haveli, Lily and I went off to check some arrangements with our guide Bilou, who'd been waiting outside the hotel gate and greeted us effusively. Bilou had approached us a couple of years previously, describing himself as the only 'officially professional' guide in Bundi. His command of English left much to be desired, and he often used quirky but vivid turns of phrase – for example, lightning he described as 'electric clouds'. But his enthusiasm and sense of humour more than made up for his limited English.

As we strolled up the narrow street, we told him of our woes with the Haveli guesthouse.

'Ah! These people very greedy, having few friends in Bundi. People saying, last month electricity company see they stealing power for many years, so now they pay big fine. This why they so unhappy with hot water!'

The reasons for the old man's obsession with the electricity were now abundantly clear.

On hearing that we were not planning on visiting Bundi again because of the lack of good accommodation, Bilou was most distraught.

'Maybe you change hotels?' he suggested. 'There is very nice place near my house, cousin of the Maharaja is running.'

We hadn't heard of this place, and it didn't rate a mention in the guidebooks, but after the horrors of the Haveli there seemed no harm in taking a look. After we had made our tour of the fort and deposited the clients back at the guesthouse, the three of us squeezed onto our motorbike and rolled down through town, with Bilou giving plentiful directions.

The Ishwari Niwas hotel was a grand old place in genteel decline, with a large pillared portico for its entrance. We liked the look of it immediately. Bilou introduced us to Mayur and his uncle Balbhadra who, together with their family, managed the establishment.

Mayur was a young man in his late twenties, slightly built and with an engaging smile. His uncle was the paternal cousin of the Maharaja of Bundi, whilst Mayur was only related on the maternal side, which evidently doesn't count at all in Rajasthan. They both seemed friendly and competent, and we agreed to a tour of the premises. Painted in pastel blues, yellows and terracottas the hotel was beautiful enough on its own, but the Bundi murals hand-painted on the walls of each room gave some idea of the artwork the village is renowned for. Bizarrely, each of the beautifully painted rooms contained a stout but ugly wardrobe with a painted sign saying 'lifejacket locker' on its front. In a city nearly a thousand kilometres from the sea this seemed an overenthusiastic precaution against drowning, unless the famed Bundi stepwells were somehow prone to overflowing in Biblical proportions.

Mayur assured us that floods were not an issue and that the lockers came from an auction in Alang on the southern coast of neighbouring Gujarat. Many of the world's worn-out ships are dragged up on the beach and dismantled in Alang, with scant regard for the environment. Hundreds of nearby auction houses peddle the detritus from these demolished cargo ships, supertankers and warships to anyone wanting an inexpensive source of furniture. Our lifejacket lockers could have come from anything from an oil tanker to a warship, and it was strange to think of such wreckage ending up in our beautiful rooms. But apart from the lifejacket locker oddity the rooms were cool, comfortable and spacious, and exuded an old-world charm.

As we shared a pot of tea in the reception area, seated on plush velvet chairs designed for more regal bottoms than ours, our negotiations were quick and simple. Mayur agreed to accommodate us at the same price as the Haveli, and assured us that they would show our clients a lot more respect and hospitality. We made immediate plans to flee the Haveli and, on our next tour, take our clients to the comfort of the Ishwari Niwas.

As we were leaving, Mayur mentioned that he had the keys to the private rooms of Bundi Palace, which housed spectacular and rarely seen murals. As special guests of his hotel we would be able to visit this area with him as a guide.

Bilou's face dropped upon hearing this, as he saw his guiding fees from our groups disappearing. For a man in his fifties, as Bilou was, this could be a catastrophic drop in income. But I didn't think it fair for Bilou to suffer financially when he'd done us the favour of finding our new accommodation, so I reassured him that some arrangement would be made.

We found out just what a huge bonus it was to have access to the palace a month later when our next group, accompanied by Mayur and Bilou, climbed up the hill to Bundi Palace for the first time. Rudyard Kipling, who was a close friend of one of the previous maharajas of Bundi and often visited the area, is often quoted as saying that 'Bundi Palace was not built by the hands of man, rather those of angels'.

We entered the palace through the enormous 'elephant gate', passing through the twenty-foot-high archway into a vast courtyard overlooked by a throne pedestal perched on a collapsing balcony. As Mayur spoke of the history and past glories of this exquisite Rajput palace his passion and love for these sadly crumbling monuments became plain. The wealth, prosperity and loyalty that had enabled the construction of this 500-room palace and surrounding fort gave us all pause for thought.

We followed the winding stairs up to the immense main throne room. Of the throne itself, only a chipped marble slab remained. As we strolled across the room a large band of black-faced monkeys awoke chattering from their afternoon sleep. They loped off casually down into the courtyard, the males glaring over their shoulders at the group of usurpers into what was definitely now their kingdom. Passing through one more locked gate and a multi-pillared courtyard, we arrived at a magnificent ivory and teak door. Stepping through the doorway we shuffled and stumbled into several dark rooms. As Mayur opened the creaking shutters a shaft of light fell on the walls. There was an audible collective gasp as the riot of colour was revealed.

Intricate painting depicting all aspects of ancient Rajput life covered every surface. Detailed vistas of battles and hunting parties spread across the full expanse of the walls, picked out in brilliant reds, greens and golds. Ominously, stains and cracks radiated from the ceilings, and in several places chunks of plaster had fallen from the walls. It was a pensive group that passed out of the gate, many of us reflecting upon the great civilisation that had been and gone here.

The palace and most of the fort remain the private property of the present Maharaja, a reclusive soul who spends much of his time in Delhi and none at Bundi Palace. Like many monuments around Rajasthan, Bundi Palace has fallen into a terrible state of disrepair. The almost impossible task of preserving this treasure has fallen to Mayur, who is working on the formation of a trust to raise money towards the maintenance of at least the painted parts of the palace.

Mayur's guiding responsibility ended at the palace gate and he took his leave. Bilou cheerfully led us up into the massive fort complex, capering along in front of us and stopping every now and then for stragglers who might have missed his explanation of the various near-derelict buildings. In his unique style – 'Ladies and gentlemens! Please! You are looking here!' – he chivvied the group up the long steep road to the summit, pausing to explain the vagaries of the medieval plumbing systems supplying the fountains below.

Along the way we passed through several gates and a couple of minor palaces and residences, all near-ruins. Legend has it that a fortune in gold and silver treasure lies hidden away in these buildings by one of the late maharajas. Over the years many opportunists have tried their luck at digging up floors or smashing down hollow walls in search of this 'Eldorado', with disastrous consequences for the fort.

As we wound our way through this marvellous, tumbledown, overgrown structure we found ourselves at the watchtower on the far southern point of the fort. The ancient and the modern clash horribly here. The current Maharaja and his sister fell out when she sold the site next to the massive 600-year-old fort to the national broadcaster, who speedily erected a hideous concrete transmission tower. Considering the sometimes sporadic nature of telecommunications in India, the main purpose of this tower is to uglify the landscape.

On the watchtower roof, however, a splendid surprise awaited us. Mayur and the entire staff of the hotel had spent the last couple of hours setting up a traditional Rajasthani picnic. Enormous rugs covered the rooftop, and several crates of beer and cold drinks sat to one side. Pots bubbled away merrily on an open wood fire as two cooks stirred the food and flipped chapatis. As the bikies reached for drinks the rest of Mayur's family arrived, and we all leaned back to admire the sun setting over the fort and valley below.

'How'd you set this one up Steve?' asked one very satisfied client. 'Another great surprise out of the hat!'

'We do our best', I grinned.

The hotel staff set large disposable plates fashioned from compressed leaves in front of us and heaped these with chapatis, several different curries and salads. As soon as the pile of food on our plates shrank even slightly, more was dished out until we begged for mercy.

By the time we'd eaten our fill, night had fallen in a moonless, starry sky. We now faced the long walk back down to the city through the ruins where Bilou had told us earlier that a leopard had been seen not a month ago. Not really wanting to lose any clients to roaming beasts or broken legs, I took Mayur aside. 'This was a brilliant idea, and everyone's had a great time – but how will we get back in the dark?'

He led me to another wall not 50 metres from our picnic and up some steps to the parapet. On the other side, another narrow staircase led down to the road to the transmission tower, where four jeeps awaited us.

'We thought you might not fancy your chances with the dark so we arranged a ride. It'll be a bit bumpy but only the first few miles', said Mayur.

Somehow we squeezed everyone and all the picnic gear into the jeeps. Several of the hotel staff hung off the sides in true Indian fashion as we bounced down the narrow track back to town, now thankful that the ugly tower and this road existed.

This time, back at the hotel after touring the palace with our seventh group, Mayur and his uncle joined us for a drink in the courtyard, bringing several old photograph albums with them. Flipping through these photos gave us a further glimpse of the opulence of life in the palace not fifty years ago and were a true measure of what had been lost. In one of the late Maharaja's wedding and investiture photos he greeted visitors arriving on elephant-back in the courtyard. In another, he sat on his lushly padded throne, the same throne that was now just a cracked marble slab. An entourage of bejewelled minions surrounded him. Rich carpets and wall hangings had adorned the rooms that we had walked through just hours before, the same rooms in which a band of monkeys now held court. It made our visit to the palace that morning all the more heart-breaking.

'My sister is getting married here at the hotel next month,' remarked Mayur as we looked through the photos. 'Tutu, the owner of the Diggi Palace Hotel in Jaipur, is to be her husband. You should come.'

Lily and I took our groups to stay at the Diggi Palace every time we visited Jaipur and we'd become good friends with Tutu, who was the nephew of the Maharaja of Diggi.

'We know Tutu well,' I said. 'He's a really nice guy. That'll be a wonderful wedding between your families.'

'Our families have been related for many centuries,' said Mayur. 'Bundi has always made alliances with other principalities. That is why Bundi has always maintained its independence and the fort has never been attacked.'

Lily and I checked the dates for the wedding. Unfortunately we would be elsewhere over the wedding period, but discovered that the reception in Jaipur would coincide with our stay there. This would be a real treat. The celebrations surrounding Hindu weddings last for several weeks, starting with the wedding proper at the bride's home. The groom, replete from several days of family feasting and surrounded by his noisy entourage, arrives on horse, or in this royal case on elephant-back complete with a band of musicians to claim his betrothed. His incredibly noisy musical procession through the bride's town takes several hours and is lit by scores of elaborate chandeliers carried by chandelier-wallahs and punctuated by the sound of fireworks exploding all around. At the ceremony's climax, the bride and groom take seven steps hand in hand around a fire. After still more feasting with the bride's family, the groom's entourage move on to his home, where a reception is held. We'd attended several Indian weddings over the years, and had even been invited to the parties, but a royal reception would surely be something special.

After breakfast the next day we took the group to see the Bundi baoris, or stepwells, starting with a short walk to the Raniji-ki Baori in the middle of town. When we arrived, the gate was locked. After we'd trawled around the perimeter for a few minutes, looking as conspicuous as a parade of circus clowns, news of our arrival reached the gatekeeper who showed up with the key. A long flight of 10-metre-wide marble steps led down to the water level, 46 metres at its deepest, descending between high marble walls carved with reliefs of deities and elephants. Even the murk and slime in the water and pigeon droppings on the marble floor didn't detract too much from the elegant symmetry of the baori, which has stood since

1699 and served as a main source of the town's water until relatively recently.

As we left the baori a woman in an orange sari stepped out of her nearby house and set a small cage trap on the ground. A large brown rat scampered out, twitched its whiskers and disappeared into the gutter. The woman carefully closed up the cage and went back indoors.

'Haven't they heard of poison!' muttered Owen, unaware that Hindus believe the rat is the constant and faithful companion of the elephant god Ganesh, the god of new beginnings and our good luck charm on the bikes. Some rat tolerance was called for.

The rest of the morning was free time for the group. Lily and I set off to visit our friend Soni Gopal, a young artist who ran a little shop up near the fort. Soni had been introduced to us as the man responsible for some of the unusual paintings in our hotel rooms, and we had commissioned a special work from him. When we mentioned this, half the group joined us on the walk through town, hoping to pick up some souvenirs.

We followed the narrow main street as it wove through a series of magnificent gates designed to offer defence to the fort. The huge town wall to our left formed one side of the busy street, and from the small rooms and cubbyholes within its structure businesses of every type plied their wares. Tinsel, bangles, brass water jugs, padlocks, pointed leather shoes, sesame snacks, packets of paan, watches, silver jewellery, silk saris, trombones, drums and cornets to rent for weddings all jostled for space within the wall. We searched high and low, but there was not a roof rack to be seen to replace our stolen one.

Down each side of the road narrow, half-open sewers flowed. Outside one shop a scabby black pig rooted around in the sewer, snout buried to the ears in the stream of filthy grey water and unidentifiable lumps.

'Municipal sanitary engineer,' called a shopkeeper, pointing at the porker and laughing at our astonished and slightly horrified faces.

'It seems to work,' said Karen, sniffing the air. 'It doesn't smell too bad. No worse than the usual piggy smell.'

An elderly blue-eyed Sikh on a bicycle stopped to chat with Lily and Karen, while Ken bought some more bottled water from a roadside shop.

'I thank you for coming to my city,' said the Sikh. 'It is comparatively very hospitable, unique and with dignity, like myself, and not tarnished by Coca-Cola.'

Ken wandered up just in time for a vigorous round of handshaking. When Ken's turn came the Sikh shook his hand, then reeled him in like a fish and kissed him juicily on his blond head. Hospitable, indeed.

'What's it like being snogged by a Sikh?' I asked Ken later.

He thought for a minute. 'It wasn't too bad. He had a nice soft beard.'

Eventually we arrived at the little art shop tucked into a corner of one of the gates near the top of town. Soni Gopal greeted us smiling with hands clasped together and ushered us all in, sitting us down on cane stools. He called to the chai-wallah next door to bring tea for everyone. A multitude of paintings in the Mughal 'Bundi-school' style of the art we'd seen at the palace covered the walls of the shop. Stylised maharajas, maharanis, concubines, warriors, gods and elephants cavorted across these finely drawn miniature paintings on paper and silk. At a small, low school desk with a cushion for a seat were all the trappings of his craft: tiny paint pots, brushes and a couple of works in progress.

When the chai had been distributed Soni pulled out an envelope and handed it to me shyly.

'This is not traditional-style work,' he giggled as we admired the painting I'd commissioned. It was a stylised rendition of a maharaja and maharani riding alongside a lotus lake with a palace in the background. What made the painting unique was that the couple was mounted on an Enfield Bullet.

'This is just what I wanted,' I enthused. 'It'll be perfect for our brochure and website.'

By this time several of our group had busied themselves among the piles of paintings on the table, admiring the works and asking if they were for sale. They were, and the prices were absurdly cheap. Quite a number of rupees and paintings changed hands over the next half hour. There was no high pressure sales spiel here, nor inflated prices in US dollars. One by one the bikies drifted off back down to the hotel, until only Lily and I were left. As we prepared to leave, Soni offered us a fairly thick wad of rupee notes.

'Your commission sir,' he said. Lily and I looked at each other, more than a little mortified. He had mistaken our desire to sit and enjoy our chai and his company for impatience to receive a kickback from our clients' sales. The commission system thrives amongst tour guides in India, many of them demanding up to fifty percent from shops on all of their clients' purchases. We'd never had anything to do with this Mafia-like scam. Much to Soni Gopal's puzzlement, we refused his money.

'We bring our clients here because we like your paintings, not for commissions,' I explained. Without too much reluctance Soni put the money back in his pocket. But when we tried to pay for our motorbike painting, he firmly refused to accept any payment.

Later that evening we again visited Bundi Palace, where we'd organised dinner for the group in the one-time elephant stables. Tables had been set up amongst the elephant hitching posts and torches lit along the walls.

'What d'you reckon,' I asked the group at my table. 'Seen enough of Bundi?'

They stared at me as if I'd just announced I was planning to build a second, even uglier, transmission tower in the middle of the fort.

'Bundi is such a cool town,' said Karen, who'd forgotten about her near-disaster and bashed leg on the ride here in the excitement of dining in such unusual surroundings. 'It'd be excellent to have another day here.'

Damn. On the last tour we'd stayed three days in Bundi, but that group had got restless on the last day so we'd shaved a day off for the next tour. Now this bunch was asking for it back.

As we strolled back down to the hotel Ken said to me, 'You know, it doesn't look as though much has changed here in the last few hundred years, apart from the electricity and petrol.'

'No, I think you're right. This is as real a window in time as anything in the world.'

When we arrived back at the hotel Mayur was waiting to settle our account. As we finished our business he handed me an ornate envelope.

'Please give this to Rao Singh when you arrive at the Hotel Castle Bijaipur. This is an invitation to all his family to my sister's wedding. Please tell him that it is most important to us that he attends.'

'They are business associates of your family?' I asked.

'Oh no! Their family and ours have many connections through many marriage alliances over the years.'

Here was yet another example of Bundi's royalty positioning itself with an eye to the future, even though their power as rulers had crumbled away just like the stones of the palace.

I tucked the invitation away safely. I didn't have to carry it very far. Bijaipur was the next stop on our tour of the royal mansions and castles of Rajasthan.

Chapter Nine

The scenery along the road from Bundi to Bijaipur shimmered like a mirage. We rode the first 50 kilometres on a fairly well-maintained but narrow two-lane country road meandering between relatively prosperous, well-watered villages. As we chugged through this bountiful landscape we met a steady trickle of milkmen travelling in the opposite direction into Bundi town. Occasionally a cloud of black smoke puffed up on the horizon, and then a rider in an orange or green turban on an overloaded motorbike would wobble out from the smoke screen, his brass jars of milk jutting out on either side.

About thirty minutes out of Bundi, we pulled over for a toilet stop as those last-minute cups of tea we'd had at breakfast made their presence felt. One of the milkmen stopped to take a closer look at these exotic aliens on bikes. To his surprise, his diesel-powered steed was of far more interest to the bikies than we were to him. I'd told the technophiles amongst the group about the unusual and economical 500cc diesel Enfield, which was just a standard Bullet with the petrol-powered cylinder and head replaced by a diesel engine, but I suspected they'd treated the story with some cynicism. Now here one was, large as life and freely available for our inspection. The group gathered around the smiling but baffled milkman and bombarded him with questions.

'What's the fuel consumption like? What's the top speed? How much milk is in there?'

The milkman boasted, 'Consumption is very good, almost one

hundred kilometres per litre of diesel. When the gods send a wind in my favour it is almost sixty-five kilometres per hour I am reaching!'

These statistics dumbfounded the bikers, particularly those who owned gas-guzzling motorcycles at home. These figures were especially impressive since the milkman carried close to 200 litres of buffalo milk in his four brass containers.

'Where do you take the milk to?' asked Neil.

'I go around the houses and people buy from me.' He showed us his half-litre brass dipper. 'Would you like to try some milk? Absolutely guaranteed to be not containing any water.'

There were no takers for this fresh, but warm and unpasteurised product.

A few minutes later we crossed a causeway over a lake and began a slow uphill climb. Over the rise, the terrain changed dramatically. There was no water on this side of the valley. The land on either side of the road was completely bare of crops, or even of soil. Great sheets of stone and exfoliated rock fragments stretched as far as the eye could see. The only sign of life in this blasted landscape was a scrawny metre-long monitor lizard. The panicked creature zigzagged along the road away from us and eventually took refuge in a lone dead tree, squinting malevolently down at us from the safety of a high branch.

Looking back at the view over the lake it was as though someone had drawn a line down the plain, and then coloured in one half of the picture but forgot the other half. Beyond this invisible line, the fertile flood plains extended towards Bundi. One could make out the monsoon level of the lake and see the dark patches where resourceful farmers had planted crops in the fertile lake bed as the waters slowly receded, confident in the wisdom of many generations that the monsoon would not replenish the water before the crops ripened.

On our side of the lake, though, there was nothing but grey stone. As we resumed our climb the few remaining trees faded out as well. At the top of the plateau a couple of forlorn pillars and a sign proclaimed that we were entering Chittorgarh district, and the desolate vista rolled endlessly on. The few villages we passed through were made up of grim stone hovels with sheets of stone for roofs and fences. They looked impoverished and almost deserted, with none of the normal bustle of village life.

Several quarries were operating along the roadside, extracting great slabs of the sandstone in the intense heat. We stopped to watch the painstaking progress of one slab from the rock face to a bullock cart. Every operation at these quarries was done by hand, with not a machine to be seen. The stone lay in straight horizontal strata, and the first job was to drive a line of spikes into the rock about a metre back from its face. With repeated strikes this eventually caused a fracture across the grain of the stone. It was then relatively simple to drive wedges in along the grain, freeing the rock.

The driving of the spikes and wedges was, however, bone-jarring work, all done without a scrap of shade in temperatures reaching the mid-thirties and more. We could almost feel the pain and weariness in the workmen's arms and shoulders as they lifted their six-kilogram sledgehammers and slammed them into the spikes. One man took five or six hits at the row, then sank exhausted to the ground as another took his place. In this way a huge block of stone one metre wide and about five metres long was separated from the face. This was quickly moved with a skilful use of rollers, wedges and crowbars to another area. There, the blocks were split along the grain into the one hundred millimetre-thick slabs used instead of scarce timber in the construction of floors and roofs in most buildings in northern India.

'The recruitment office is over there if any of you fancy a career change at fifty rupees a day,' I said in a very dry and unsuccessful attempt at humour, pointing towards a small stone shack.

We were all obviously suffering from the heat after standing out in this sun for just twenty minutes. It was sobering to imagine doing hard physical work in these temperatures.

The wind in our faces revived us as we rode the last hour to Bijaipur through the desert wasteland. As we turned at a sign announcing 'Hotel Castle Bijaipur' and headed up a river valley the countryside instantly, and almost miraculously, became green again, with well-tended fields and more affluent villages and hamlets.

At the final river crossing the sixteenth century castle loomed into breathtaking view. With its domed turrets and overhanging balconies it looked like a giant wedding cake sprouting from the centre of the village. Snaking through the dusty village streets we approached the twenty-foot-high walls and entered through the enormous and imposing double gateway, rattling the cattle-stop as we crossed. As we pulled up inside the entrance under the shade of the trees and removed our helmets, there were gasps of amazement at this Garden of Eden of green lawns, roses and palm trees.

The staff had dressed in traditional Rajasthani costume and formed a welcoming party outside the main entrance. Rao Singh, the owner of the hotel, strode over and shook our hands, then ushered our clients towards the receiving line to have marigold and rose garlands draped around their necks and tika spots dotted on their foreheads. Six feet tall, thickset and with a broad moustache curled up impressively at the ends, Rao Singh was a formidable figure. His family had lived in this castle for thirteen generations and had a great reputation for bravery. They had been granted the area by the Maharaja of Udaipur in return for defending his realm from the aggressive Malwar tribes just over the hill. The old part of the castle was built with defence in mind with steep stairways, low narrow doorways and small easily defended rooms.

Lily took on the tricky job of allocating the rooms. This delicate task required the wisdom of Solomon to ensure that no one felt they'd been short-changed throughout the journey. I went with Rao Singh to visit his family in the private wing of the castle and handed over the wedding invitation that Mayur had entrusted to us in Bundi. They offered me a cup of amul dasdur, a sweetened milky drink laced with a small amount of opium, a traditional welcome for a guest in any Rajasthani house in this area. I politely refused and opted for a much safer cup of chai. While we sipped our drinks we chatted about the plans for this important wedding and how Lily and I hoped to be at the reception in Jaipur in a week's time.

After abandoning their belongings in their rooms the bikers set about exploring every part of the castle open to them and comparing accommodation. Karen and Ken thought they'd been lucky to get 'The Love Room', as Lily described it, a sizeable marble-floored room of arched doorways, yellow and orange lead-light shutters and carved wooden doors fastened by brass padlocks. Others had been given equally spacious rooms set off a long marble balcony furnished at each end with padded swing seats suspended from chains of brass horses and camels. A nearly life-sized plaster tiger greeted guests in one of these rooms.

But it was generally agreed that Matt and Owen had drawn the long straw. Lily had felt, quite correctly, that these two lone males had missed out on some of the better rooms at other locations, so she'd given them a suite taking up the entire top floor of the old part of the castle. Once this news spread amongst the group there was a small stampede up the narrow, winding staircase to view these new splendours. Owen and Matt took turns giving guided tours of their palatial accommodation, starting at the red carpet of the receiving room and leading past the matching red velvet chairs, some with lions' heads for arms, and carrying on through the ornately carved marble pillars into the magnificent antechamber. At either end of the antechamber were the two domed-ceilinged bedrooms, hung with draperies and paintings of Rajput ancestors.

The elevated cushion-covered recess off the antechamber overlooked the castle gardens and the farmlands beyond, making a perfect venue for a couple of drinks. Soon there was a well-lubricated hubbub echoing through the ancient building as the castle waiters rushed to and fro supplying cold beers.

Lily and I followed the noise and joined the group with our bottle of gin and the more valuable tonic water.

'Help yourselves to the gin but take it easy on the tonic!' I warned. 'Believe it or not, it's almost impossible to buy "Indian tonic water" over here. We had to bring these cans all the way from Thailand.'

Once the novelty of the suite wore off, some of the group wandered up onto the roof. From there we had an almost voyeuristic look into life in the village directly below, and a wide view of the surrounding countryside stretching as far as the distant Aravalli

Range. A woman bent over a steaming pile of cow dung, shaping it into patties, while other women on rooftops hung silk saris out to dry.

'What were all those fields of white flowers that we passed on the last bit of the ride?' asked Alex, pointing out to a couple of fields beyond the castle wall.

'This valley is one of the biggest state-controlled opium growing areas in the world. We'll get a chance to visit one of the opium fields tomorrow.'

At dusk a bell sounded for dinner, and there was a bit of a frenzy at the buffet laid out in the front courtyard. Goat curry was on the menu. Most of the group, more than a little wary of contracting some fearful contagion, had eaten very little meat since the start of the tour. I assured them that this goat had died in our honour this morning and was safe to eat. After the goat curry pot had been emptied, the bones sucked and the plates licked clean, we all sat back to enjoy the dancing and music performed for us by the castle staff. A slim figure in an elaborate red sari twisted and twirled to the beat of the tabla drums, while one of the musicians sang stories of village life.

After a few moments Karen sat forward in her chair.

'Hmmm,' she said, 'that's not a woman up there dancing.'

'Yes it is! What are you talking about?' demanded Owen and Ken, who'd both been admiring the dancer's gyrations.

'That's definitely not a woman,' insisted Karen. 'I've watched the Indian women walking along. They've got more grace in one finger than that person has in their whole body. Sorry guys, but that's a young man in drag.'

Owen and Ken protested long and loudly that the lithe, lovely figure before them was a woman, not a man. Bets were made, and I was sent off to ask Rao Singh to resolve the situation.

Rao Singh confirmed that, yes, it was a man, adding that it would be quite inappropriate, if not scandalous, for a village woman to dance in public. There was a bit of murmuring and brow-mopping among the disbelieving menfolk while Karen collected her winnings.

As we watched the dancer's finale Rao Singh stood to one side, winding a 10-metre length of coloured cloth into a turban. Once the turban was wound completely atop his head Rao Singh looked every inch a royal, perhaps not surprising for someone who was a descendent of the Rajput warrior Shakti Singh, younger brother of the famous Maharaja Pratap Singh. With a regal flourish Rao Singh lifted the turban from his own head and set it on mine. The titters and snorts from the group left me in no doubt that I didn't cut quite the same princely figure.

Despite the long day's ride and the extended cocktail hour nobody was ready for bed. The group discussed several entertainment options, including a few more drinks in Matt and Owen's quarters. Luckily the two bikers were saved from having the entire crowd camped out all night in their anteroom by the sounds of far more interesting happenings outside the castle walls. The theatre had arrived in the village.

Dalpat, the manager of the hotel, offered to accompany us into the village to see this 'cultural programme'.

'The village would be most honoured if you would attend,' he assured us.

Most of the group eagerly took Dalpat up on the offer. Bringing our torches as directed we stumbled through the unlit village streets, occasionally surprising a wandering cow or stepping in some unidentifiable wetness. Eventually we blundered out of the darkness into a large square. What seemed to be the entire population of Bijaipur, men, women and children, sat crammed together on the dirt floor of the square. All eyes were fixed upon us. A path magically opened through the crush of the crowd, and we made our way toward a spot near the back. A couple of men manhandled several charpoys out of an adjoining house and offered them to us.

With the 'guests of honour', as we seemed to be, all comfortably seated, everybody's attention switched back to the brightly-lit stage in the middle of the square where the performers had been patiently awaiting an end to the competing spectacle of our entrance. Four outlandishly garbed actors cavorted on stage, two men and two brassy 'women'. By now we'd learned a lesson from our dancer of earlier in the evening, and there were no arguments about who was what. These performers were of the Bhand caste, who travel around the countryside entertaining in small villages such as Bijaipur and relying upon the generosity of the villagers to eke out a living. The small group of musicians punctuated each actor's speech with wild riffs on the tabla and cranks of the hurdy-gurdy accompanied by a harmonium, while clowns in black and white face paint wheedled donations from the crowd.

Although the dramatic speeches were completely unintelligible to us, the general plot was clear. With copious amounts of drink and her feminine wiles, a wanton woman of the night lured an honest farmer away from his work and family to certain ruin. Eventually, the repentant farmer discovered the error of his ways and, with the help of a noble prince, returned to his family. To make the plot nice and neat the prince married the now-reformed woman, making her a princess.

This characteristically Indian melodrama unfolded amid gasps and shrieks from the audience at the disgraceful flirting and hip-flouncing. After an hour or so it was obvious that the show could go on for quite some time, and the crowd had much more stamina for staying up late than we did. After making a donation to one of the clowns we took our leave into the blackness of the village.

The itinerary was free for the following morning, so after the usual eggs and toast the group wandered off to find comfortable, shady spots to read and relax. A group of women trailed into the inner garden and, settling on the lawn, began to hack away at the grass with short knives while they chattered amongst themselves.

'Indian lawn mower,' explained Rao Singh's daughter, Prianka. 'They come and cut this grass for us, and then they get to keep the cuttings for feeding their animals.'

There were surprised mutterings at this ridiculously slow and tedious method.

'Why don't you get a machine?' asked one biker. 'You'd get it done in a tenth of the time.'

'That would save time, yes, but then where would these women get animal food, and where would they be able to gather to talk freely outside their homes?' Yet again the obvious here wasn't so obvious to us.

'Would any of the gentlemen like a shave or haircut?' she continued. 'The village barber is closed today, as Tuesday is a forbidden day for Hindus to cut their hair. But none of you are Hindu, so he will come here and perform this service.'

Half an hour later the barber, with his well-worn chair and a small mirror had set up shop under a pomegranate tree in the garden. A queue of clients sat waiting for him to prove my guarantee that a shave at an Indian barber is one of the finest luxuries a man could partake in. To reassure some of the sceptics I took the first turn.

I lay back in the chair while a thick soapy lather was briskly worked up on my face. Then the stubble was carefully scraped off with a straight razor. In times gone past, these razors were honed and stropped to a fine edge, but in these times of various blood-borne diseases a nifty little razor-blade holder is used, with a new disposable blade inserted for each client. Just when I thought that even the tiniest whisker had been chased down and removed, the barber lathered me up again and scraped my face one more time. He then applied a liberal splashing of antiseptic alcohol and vigorously massaged my entire head. Finally, he rubbed my face with an astringent alum stone. As always, I got up from this ten-rupee experience refreshed and glowing. Soon the barber was doing a brisk business.

With most of the men in the group shaved clean and considerably tidier it was time for our visit to the opium fields. Rao Singh insisted on riding with me, so with him riding pillion we set off up the valley. It quickly became apparent that my passenger was a Very Important Person in this area and he was shown great deference by all we passed.

The title of Rao signifies the chieftainship over some eighty villages, and until independence this entire area was run through a system of minor Rajput officials who administered every detail of village life. After India's independence from the British, much of the family land was claimed by the government. But even today Rao Singh is still often called upon in preference to the courts to resolve village disputes.

On all sides people stopped what they were doing and stared open-mouthed at our group and then, recognising Rao Singh, placed their hands together in namaskar, the traditional and still very current mark of respect, which he was constantly returning. At one point we were stuck behind a slow-moving, exhaust-spewing bus on the narrow road and people looking out of the back window waved in the customary manner. Suddenly, one of the passengers recognised my passenger and ran up to the front of the bus, which almost immediately pulled off the road to allow us past in an unheard of display of courtesy.

After riding in this regal procession for about 10 kilometres, we pulled up in a small village. A ripple of excitement spread through the village, starting with a group of wide-eyed children and eventually reaching the village headman, who emerged from his home rubbing his eyes. Over his shoulder he carried an ancient and rusty shotgun which looked equally dangerous for the user or intended victim. As he respectfully greeted Rao Singh he kept one still-sleepy eye on us. It wasn't clear which sight he found more astonishing.

After a few words with our guide, the headman relaxed and agreed to accompany us to one of the fields. Leaving our bikes blocking the village street we set off along a narrow path through the poppies.

We'd arrived at harvest time, the busiest season. During this time every grower and their families worked in the fields from dawn to dusk gathering the crop. For the entire six-week harvest period, open-sided huts thatched with palm leaves became home for these farming families. We stopped at one field where the poppies had lost their white flowers and grown billiard-ball-sized seed heads. One of the growers abandoned his work long enough to take us amongst the crop and demonstrate the labour-intensive process to us.

Grasping one of the poppies, he made a series of shallow cuts in the seed head with a special four-bladed knife to make the head bleed. He explained through Rao Singh that this was highly skilled work: if the cuts are too deep, the pink milk oozes back inside the seed head, and if they're too shallow very little milk seeps out. His job the next morning, when the sticky milk had set and darkened, would be to scrape the raw brown opium off the head with a different curved knife, yielding about half a gram of the sticky goo per flower. One day of harvesting by the family, we were told, produced around two kilograms of raw opium.

Opium in the Bijaipur area is theoretically all grown under government licensing control. Every licensee is entitled to grow one hectare of opium poppies. For this privilege the grower is under contract to sell fifty-five kilograms of opium to government buyers. In a good year, one hectare of poppies will produce up to ninety kilograms of opium. The government price for opium is around 5000 rupees per kilogram, whereas the black market rate is four times that amount. It is quite possible that some of this excess does not find its way to the government buyers.

Time was pressing on, so we departed from the fields and continued on our journey through the valley, back to the castle. On the way it seemed that on every hilltop, no matter how insignificant, the ruins of some fortification looked down on us, like ghosts from the warring past of this valley.

We arrived back in the village just on dusk where another sumptuous meal awaited, this time served on the roof of the new castle overlooking the moonlit village and valley. The castle's entire inventory of crockery and cutlery, as well as low seats and a large number of rugs, had been laboriously carried up to this third-floor rooftop just to serve our dinner. This would all be carried down again in time for breakfast.

As we enjoyed our pre-dinner drinks, watching the moon rise over the hills, Matt said, 'This would be one of the most romantic hotels in the world. I think I'll come back here for my honeymoon.'

I couldn't help but agree with him. Although Lily and I had stayed here many times, the romance of Bijaipur Castle never dimmed. We'd be sad to leave in the morning for the trip to Chittorgarh and Udaipur.

Chapter Ten

Chittorgarh is one of the most ancient and extensive forts in Rajasthan, and occupies a ridge 12 kilometres long. On the ride up from the old city through the seven fortified gates the foreboding battlements give an inkling of how arduous it must have been for the warriors who sacked this fort three times. Many of the palaces and temples inside have long since fallen to ruin.

By the time we arrived in Chittorgarh many of our group had had enough of ancient history. After a token poke around a tumbledown palace or two, most of them gave up pretending to be interested in the melancholy tale of the fort's previous inhabitants and bolted straight for a row of street hawkers crowding one end of the fort complex.

Bargaining hard, they fell upon the tatty offerings as if they'd never seen cheap souvenirs before. Toy wooden camels, peacocks and tigers with bobbing heads, tinny perfume bottles on chains, wretchedly hideous plastic necklaces; all this and scads of other short-lived junk disappeared by the bagful. As Matt explained, 'I just want to get the trinket-buying over with.' This seemed to be the rallying cry for the other shoppers as they rampaged from stall to stall, determined to fulfil their souvenir-buying obligations no matter how dire the stuff on offer.

Trinket-buying is hard work, though, so we stopped for cold drinks at a chai-stand playing catchy Indian tunes on a portable cassette player. We settled ourselves on benches and chairs, and a thin man limped out to take our orders. Instead of going round the group and counting up the numbers of colas, lime sodas or mineral waters, he asked each person for their order individually. Each time he limped up and down the aisle we cringed sympathetically. After his umpteenth trip the music suddenly changed to Michael Jackson singing 'Little Drummer Boy', presumably in our honour. This was enough to send the entire group fleeing out of the shop once they'd finished their drinks.

The short rest revived us enough to visit a temple a short distance down the road. When we emerged from the temple it was clear that word had got out about this bunch of big spenders. The number of vendors had tripled, and this time included small children selling hand-drawn postcards and some threadbare handbags. One man peddling booklets of Kama Sutra postcards, including one demonstrating a man in intimate congress with a donkey, did a roaring trade.

With the group's shopping needs satisfied, at least temporarily, we seized the chance to herd them back onto the road. Our next stop was Udaipur, one of the most beautiful, romantic and busy cities in Rajasthan.

The road from Chittorgarh to Udaipur is one of the best rides of the journey. Two lanes of good quality tarseal with little traffic was quite a contrast to what we had been used to on the previous rides. After getting over their initial surprise the lead riders on the road tentatively wound their bikes up and travelled a fair portion of the trip at a relatively fast 85 kilometres per hour.

Udaipur was by far the biggest city we'd entered as a group. There were some tense moments as Lily and I tried to keep all the bikes together when we reached the crowded city streets. No sooner would we get everyone tightly together in a tidy line with everyone in each other's sight, than a bus or truck would force its way into the middle of the group, or start overtaking the line and breaking it up. By a combination of Lily and me riding very slowly and waiting at the front, and Ratan in the Sumo blocking any interfering traffic at the rear, we eventually arrived at our destination with a full complement.

Our hotel in Udaipur, the Mahendra Prakesh, is a peaceful haven. All the rooms open onto a shady courtyard that leads to a garden surrounding a large tiled swimming pool. The hotel is owned by Ajay Singh who, unsurprisingly, is distantly related to the Singhs of Bundi and Bijaipur. He and his manager Lala run a very relaxed and friendly establishment, and Lily and I always looked forward to arriving at this little home away from home at the mid-point of the tour. Once we'd got the clients settled in their rooms, I went down into the garden to pay a visit to a small but much-loved animal friend.

ॐ

In a petrol station near Dhausa on one of our previous trips I'd spied a strikingly patterned tortoise the size of a soup bowl rumbling around on a tiny piece of dry grass enclosed by a low brick wall, vainly searching for an exit.

'What are you feeding this animal?' I asked the petrol station manager, anxious for this endearing creature's welfare.

'This tortoise, living in desert, not eating,' he said, shaking his head at my evident naivety in tortoise affairs.

Prospects did not look good for this unfortunate chelonian if left here to starve. I remembered that Ajay had a well-fed and loved female specimen of the same species freely roaming in his hotel garden at Udaipur. This little fellow was a male. The solution seemed obvious, and I explained my plan to the manager.

'Will you sell this tortoise?' I asked him.

'Ah yes sir', he smiled, 'five hundred rupees only.'

'I'll give you one hundred, not a rupee more', I replied in mock disgust at his outrageous demand and walked off. As we were about to depart, he came up to me, holding out the tortoise.

'Take him to his marriage please', he laughed, and refused any payment whatsoever.

We then had the problem of getting Terry, as we named him, all the way from Dhausa to Udaipur, some 700 kilometres and eight days' travel away. A cardboard mineral water box was produced and a layer of straw placed in its base. I was carefully wedging it on the floor of the Sumo when Lily spotted me. She was well aware of my past life in South Africa, where I'd spent those two years as curator of Durban Snake Park, and of my intense interest in all things scaly and creepy-crawly.

'You're a real sucker for any reptile. What's the story with this one then?'

'We're on a mission of love.' I explained the reason for our new group mascot. I assured her that there would be no problems getting Terry to Udaipur. We could let him roam around the hotel gardens along the way, and it would be paramount to a death sentence to leave him languishing in Dhausa.

Soon we were back on the road with our speeding tortoise, who did not seem particularly happy about this new turn of events in his life. He spent much of his time barging around his box seeking an exit. Over the next few days our efforts to house and feed him became the source of tolerant amusement to many of the staff in the hotels we stayed in, but they all helped, providing succulent pieces of tomato and banana for his meals.

At Bijaipur Castle, though, Terry was the cause of a most undesirable reptilian encounter. We'd housed him in a small area of walled-off garden just next to the outdoor restaurant where he'd happily lumbered around, pausing to snack on the various flowers and plants within. Just before breakfast I'd gone down to check on him, as he wasn't obviously visible.

I began to rummage around in a small patch of greenery next to a tree. Twenty years of living in snake-free New Zealand had naturally mellowed my caution about putting my hands in snakey places, but something made me think of the potential danger just in time. As I pulled my hand back there was a rustle and a hiss as a small cobra reared his head from the undergrowth, hood fully spread in its most aggressive 'leave me alone' posture.

'Shit!' exclaimed a horrified client as I leapt nimbly back onto the lawn. 'You don't want to mess with that little bugger!'

Despite the very real danger from a lethal dose of cobra venom my first instinct, as an old snake-catcher from way back, was to get a closer look at this magnificent little fellow. I was ill-equipped for a snake capture, with no stick of any kind, no shoes and wearing only my longhi with nothing on underneath. Picking up a nearby piece of firewood, with one hand holding up my longhi and my bare feet well back, I poked around in the greenery. The cobra of course was getting pretty irritated by this time and decided to make a break for it. Fast as lightning it slithered straight between my legs and, with a final hiss, disappeared down a tiny hole amongst some tree roots. Why it didn't take a nip at my exposed feet as it passed by is still a mystery.

'I think we'll probably be best off leaving it alone now,' I said, barely able to conceal the shakiness in my voice.

Just then I spied Terry, oblivious to the recent drama, emerging from his resting place under the shrubs near the cobra hole and starting to search for another snack of tomato. I scooped him up and made a pretty speedy exit myself from cobra territory.

Despite these adventures we'd managed to deliver Terry safe and sound to Udaipur.

On this trip to Udaipur, we were relieved and pleased to see that Terry had become a contented though slightly frustrated resident of the Mahendra Prakesh. He spends his days dutifully following his new love, Ajay's somewhat larger lady tortoise, around the gardens of the hotel. He has as yet been unable to consummate the marriage owing to his smaller size, but he is eating everything put in front of him in a desperate effort to reach the required dimensions to finally be able to mount his mate.

With Terry's health assured, we could now concentrate on showing Udaipur to our clients. The city has a more affluent feel than most others we visit in Rajasthan, but like any place in India, it's full of surprises. Veiled women carry on their heads jugs of water drawn from a communal well, right beside signs advertising high-speed internet connections. The narrow streets and bazaars of the old city are thronged with handicraft shops, 'art schools', bookstores and, of course, cows. Portraits of Bollywood stars – and, inexplicably, Elvis – adorn autorickshaw mudflaps.

On arrival in Udaipur the group's seemingly insatiable shopping frenzy switched into high gear. When I suggested a visit to the City

Palace and Museums, the mumbles and grunts from the group gave the distinct impression that they were far more interested in the retail wares of Udaipur than in its cultural and architectural attractions. After the small rural towns where we'd spent much of our time, Udaipur was a tourist metropolis bursting with shops peddling silver and gold jewellery, silk saris in every hue, turbans, carpets and clothes. And, of course, the miniature paintings – some good, some not so good – hawked relentlessly by every shopkeeper in Udaipur.

There was no point in trying to persuade this lot to sightsee when they obviously still had shopping on their minds. Lily and I, while trying not to be too 'tour-leaderish', gave them some guidelines on what we thought were fair prices for the goods for sale. The early birds in the group discovered a shopping tip: the first customer of the day is considered to be 'good luck', so it pays to get up before the crowds. After that, the bartering is full on, and the shopkeepers are masters of the hard sell.

Karen had her eye on silver bracelets and she and Ken hit the shops early. Lily and I came along to watch the show.

'For you, madam, good price,' said one silver-peddler, spreading out a lapis lazuli bracelet. 'Five hundred rupees.'

'Three hundred,' Karen countered wildly.

'But madam, this is very fine jewellery. Real silver, ninety-two and a half percent, real stone. See?'

He whipped the bracelet off the glass case. Then, with the flourish of a true showman, he slid the bracelet back and forth over his thick thatch of well-lubricated hair.

'Four hundred,' said Karen, obviously dazzled by this display.

'Done,' said the shopkeeper, although what or who had been

'done' wasn't exactly clear. Karen paid the money and fled before he could offer her any miniature paintings. In the next shop they stumbled into yet another of the pitfalls of shopping in India.

'Very sorry sir, but I am not taking this note.'

The shop owner stared at Ken's fifty-rupee note as if it were a dead rat. To a casual inspection, it looked like any other fifty-rupee note – ridiculously thin, grubby, limp and holed at one end.

'Why not?' Ken demanded. 'It's the same as the others I've just given you.'

'Oh, no sir, is not the same. Look – here is rip –' He pointed to a tiny tear at one edge. We all had to squint to see it. 'I am not taking note with rip, very sorry sir.'

Ken pulled out another grimy, limp, holey note, scrutinised it for rips, however minuscule, and handed it over.

'Thank you sir!' The shopkeeper beamed, obviously very relieved.

It soon became clear why. A ripped rupee note is like a bad reputation. Once you've got it, it can be yours for life.

In Rajasthan, the opportunities to change foreign currency into rupees are few and far between, and the number of shops accepting credit cards can be counted on the fingers of one hand. In isolated places like Bundi and Chittorgarh Lily and I had discovered that there was no way to change any sort of foreign currency into rupees, much less get a cash advance on a credit card. On our first trip to Bundi we'd spent a completely fruitless morning being sent from bank to bank trying to change a single American hundred-dollar bill. Udaipur, with its abundance of currency exchange booths, was the first chance for our spendthrift bikers to become solvent again.

After changing what seemed like a modest sum of foreign money, many of our group had slabs of rupee notes tucked in their money belts. It's perfectly acceptable to hand a shopkeeper a filthy note with a gaping staple-hole in it. But a note with a rip along the edge is considered highly suspect, as it may have been stolen by some light-fingered thief sneaking it out of the middle of the stapled bundle of one hundred notes.

'Is there any way to fix this rupee note?' pleaded Ken with the fifth shopkeeper to turn away the note.

The shopkeeper held it up, turning it this way and that. His friend, slouched by the till, peered at it, too.

'I will see.'

Smoothing down the worn note, he joined the edges of the rip together with a small piece of tape. He then dipped the note into a jug of water standing near the till. Once the note had partially dried he dipped it again and smoothed down the rip. Much to everyone's surprise, the rip stuck together.

'Here sir, is fixed,' pronounced the shopkeeper.

'Many thanks,' Ken said, already plotting how to dispose of the note.

'Is no problem,' said the shopkeeper. 'You like to see miniature painting?'

We refused as politely as possible, backing out of the shop with the still-damp note dangling from Ken's fingers. As we turned to leave, we caught sight of the shopkeeper's friend taking a long thirsty swig from the jug of water just used to wash the ragged rupee note.

Shopping opportunities in Udaipur are only outnumbered by the eateries. A multitude of cafés cook up a variety of Westernised dishes alongside traditional Indian meals, and several 'German bakeries' offer apple pie and wholemeal bread. Flashy signs at several restaurants and cafés in the old bazaar advertise 'Dinner and "Octopussy" at 7.30 pm'. The 1960s James Bond movie was largely filmed in and around Udaipur, and the locals have been dining out on this legacy ever since.

There were several takers for this 'cultural experience' on our first night in Udaipur. From our seats at one of the rooftop eateries we kept one eye on Roger Moore as he sashayed his way through a cardboard cut-out of India on a television screen. We kept the other eye on the 'movie set' spread out below us – the exquisite Lake Palace, which featured prominently as a posh casino and hotel in the movie, and the faraway Monsoon Palace, where the bad guys plotted their evil schemes. There was definitely a 'love it or hate it' response from our bikers to this surreal and kitschy outing.

The next night the entire group went out for a thali, India's equivalent of fast food, at one of our favourite Udaipur restaurants, Nataraj. After a five-minute ride with all of us crammed 'Indian style' into the Sumo, and then a short walk a couple of hundred metres down a narrow alleyway, we all filed into this culinary gem. Once again – the grimier the external appearance, the better the quality of the food, and the exterior of this place was *very* grimy.

Before we'd even had time to sit down the waiters had already plunked a large stainless-steel plate in front of each of us. The delicious meal of rice, chapatis, pickles, onions, vegetable curries and dhals was served at a rapid pace. The multitude of waiters, each wearing the Nataraj 'corporate wardrobe' consisting of a dingy longhi and even grubbier singlet, rapidly fired the various components of the meal onto our plates. It took a while for the group to catch on to the idea of the thali – food came continuously onto the plate unless the diner waved it away. The faster we ate, the faster the food came. By the time we realised we'd eaten enough, it was way too late. We were completely, painfully full.

The entire meal cost each of us thirty-five rupees.

In complete contrast, for the next evening's meal we'd arranged for the group to have a night of eating extravagance at the Lake Palace Hotel. This exotic building takes up all the space on Jag Niwas Island in the middle of Lake Pichola, where it 'floats' like a midsummer night's dream. The Lake Palace was a royal summer residence until the 1960s when, like several of the other palace-cum-hotels where we'd stayed, it was converted into up-market accommodation.

Anticipation of this evening's event was high throughout the day amongst the group. Many shopped for shirts and sari dresses to wear, and spent several hours preparing. All fresh and looking our most suave, we set off to the jetty to take the small boat across to the palace. Puttering across the still lake at twilight toward the graceful white palace was an enchanting start.

Stepping out of the boat, we stepped back into the opulent excesses of the time of the Raj. Red-turbaned and uniformed doormen bowed us through the marble entrance, into a palm-fringed lounge attended by yet more red-turbaned waiters. The various imbibers in the group took advantage of the Palace's liquor licence, and soon margaritas, wine and, of course, gin and tonics appeared on tables everywhere.

'Think you could get used to the lap of luxury?' I asked Warren as he lounged in a cane chair sipping his margarita.

'It's all very nice but it's a bit weird,' he answered, 'especially when you know what's on the other side of the water.'

Above
Steve and Lily meet the pot-smoking potter en route to Ranakpur.

Right
Worshippers at the Jain temple, Ranakpur.

KAREN GOA

Above
Driving with the top down on the road to Pushkar.

Left
Girl with goat.

Opposite
A sadhu (holy man).

STEVE KRZYSTYNIAK

A top-heavy Tata truck loses its load.

Women from Ranthambhore Fort Village.

Despite my warning that the ritzy hotel shops had highly inflated prices in US dollars, Owen headed straight for them. Minutes later he came back, shaking his head.

'It's too rich for my blood. I've seen the same stuff in town for a quarter of the price.'

In a nearby open air theatrette the hotel's entertainment troupe charmingly balanced pots on their heads and danced to the applause of an enthusiastic crowd, who'd obviously never seen a little gypsy girl balance brass water jugs on her head while walking on a tightrope strung up on a dusty village street.

Many of the hotel patrons had dressed in their best 'going to meet the maharaja' suits, and they were a better diversion than the official entertainment. They had an air of haughty longing as they strode about the hotel brandishing their walking canes, as if they wished all the riff-raff would vanish and leave them to relive the memories of a grander era. It was almost a shame when we were called into dinner.

Faced with a lavish buffet of countless main dishes, both vegetarian and non-vegetarian, with salads and hugely calorific desserts, everyone in the group threw all caution to the wind and made sure they ate their 750 rupees' worth. It seemed fairly certain that a hotel of this calibre wouldn't poison their clientele with dodgy meat, so once again the carnivores had a feast.

It was a very bloated and drowsy crowd that got in the boat to go back to shore after dinner, and we bade each other good night much earlier than usual. Shopping and gluttony had tired everyone out.

In the morning, though, there was a fresh burst of energy after a good night's sleep. Once again the shops were under siege. Owen was on the hunt for gifts for his womenfolk, and no silver or sari shop was safe from his attentions. Lily and I sat on the street with some of the group for a while, people-watching and chatting with the shopkeepers. Every so often Owen would stagger by, weighed down by a dozen more saris or ten new bracelets and declaring, 'This is it! No more shopping!' Then ten minutes later he'd be back, hot on the trail of some little shop where someone else had got a bargain.

I watched all this with a large amount of amusement but also a small amount of alarm. We still hadn't found a roof rack to replace the one stolen earlier in the tour, and the luggage wasn't getting any smaller.

'I think we'd better take this bunch away before they buy the whole city', I said to Lily.

It was time to say goodbye to Ajay, good luck to Terry, corral the shoppers and get back on the bikes.

Chapter Eleven

After a six-thirty breakfast served and eaten by a bleary-eyed bunch, we said our last farewells to Udaipur. Once again, the Bullets started with a satisfying roar, and the group fell in line behind our lead bike.

Since all of them had managed to eat breakfast, pack their luggage and look reasonably alert by seven-thirty I decided to lead them out of Udaipur on the narrow lane winding through the old bazaar, rather than taking the faster but less interesting main road. As the line of Bullets rumbled up the cobbled street through the slowly awakening old city, the few residents up and about at this ridiculously early hour for India stopped in their tracks to stare open-mouthed at the spectacle. Our parade of Westerners never failed to flabbergast the locals, even in a relatively tourist-savvy city like Udaipur.

Traffic was light in the city, but as we turned onto the open road it slowly increased as men, women and children set out on their way to work. Buses with their roofs crammed with waving commuters careered towards us, their multi-tone air-horns screeching madly. Dozens of little scooters, some with entire families of five astride, wobbled through the melee of wagons and rickshaws. A couple of keen young men on scooters joined our convoy for a short while, thrashing their little machines badly in their attempts to keep up.

A few kilometres along we took the side road to Ranakpur, where we planned to visit a Jain temple. The road immediately shrank to one slim lane, and the traffic trickled away to the occasional overloaded jeep taxi and ox-drawn wagon. As we drove deeper into the tribal area the road surface deteriorated, the asphalt crumbling away until there was more pothole than road.

Although the landscape seemed less stark than the barren wastelands we'd driven through a few days earlier, it was still very dry and brown. Stunted trees struggled to maintain a foothold in the rocky soil, but every now and then an irrigated valley green with crops of either wheat or channa brightened the view. Electricity hadn't reached this very rural area, so irrigation by electric pump was not remotely an option. The green valleys seemed even more miraculous when we realised that any irrigating had to be done by hand, drawing water from ancient oxen-driven chain-bucket wells.

We stopped by one of these wells and dismounted for a closer look. A pair of oxen tethered to a horizontal wheel strolled around in an endless circle. As we approached, a bearded old red-turbaned man sitting sleepily on the oxen draw-bar languidly urged on the beasts in their never-ending journey. The oxen powered a crude gearing system attached to a continuous chain of earthenware pots secured on two hand-woven ropes. As the oxen circled the wheel the ropes dipped into the water at the bottom of the well, filling the pots. The pots tracked up the rope chain, emptied the water into an irrigation ditch, then continued back down into the well.

The furious click-click of shutters as the bikers recorded this scene from another era added a modern counterpoint to the slow deliberate clomp of the oxen and the swish and slop of the gently surging water.

'He's taking all day to do what an electric pump would do in half an hour!' exclaimed Warren.

Ratan, perplexed by our fascination with such a commonplace

and primitive scene, laughed aloud, sputtering, 'But he *has* all day!'

The curious crowd of Westerners climbing all over the well had stopped all irrigation work. A little fearfully, the old farmer asked Ratan, 'What do they want? Are they from the government?'

Ratan assured the farmer that no, we weren't from the government, and that we were just there to admire his magnificent well and oxen. Hearing this, he offered his seat to Neil, who never turned down an opportunity to oust the locals from their work. After a little bit of 'Giddup' and 'Get along' he got the beasts going at a fine clip.

While Neil performed with the oxen, I'd been inspecting some of the broken tulip-shaped pots from the well. The farmer, noticing my interest in his pots, beckoned us up the hill to show us the crude potter's wheel set up on the ground outside his hut. The wheel was nothing more than a flat circular stone one metre in diameter pivoting on a small wooden base. Taking up a long stick the farmer prodded the wheel until it whirled at a speed fast enough to turn clay into pot, to the awe of some of the potters in the group accustomed to getting much less impressive results from more sophisticated machinery.

'Would he sell me one of the pots?' I asked Ratan. Ratan shook his head, despairing of my ludicrous souvenir-purchasing habits, and entered into a protracted haggling session with the farmer on my behalf.

'Five rupee,' he finally pronounced, and the deal was done.

Relieved that he'd had some assistance in his day's toil, and made a profit as well, the farmer stretched out on his charpoy. Taking up a handful of green weed he stuffed it into a clay chillum. After lighting this he offered it to all of the group, then blissfully puffed away.

'Is he smoking what I think he's smoking?' asked Ken.

'Yes sir, this man is drug addict, smoking charras every day,' replied Ratan.

By the time we'd walked down the hill and started the bikes, the farmer was stretching out in preparation for a sleep.

All along the road we passed groups of shaven-headed Jains walking to or from their pilgrimages to the Ranakpur temples, wearing red robes and carrying bright red banners. They seemed in uniformly high spirits and waved and greeted us enthusiastically.

After climbing steadily for 20 kilometres through a series of narrow gorges, we emerged at the top of a vast high-walled valley cleaving through the mountains. Down the valley we could see the road clinging to sheer rock walls as it wound down towards our destination. In the far distance, the temple complex and lakes shimmered through the haze.

The Jain temple at Ranakpur is one of the most ornate in Rajasthan, and one of the most extensive of its kind in India. Founded around 500 BC, the Jain religion has elements of both Buddhism and Hinduism. Its followers are strict vegetarians, many of whom go to quite extraordinary lengths to avoid harming any living thing, even avoiding harmful thoughts. The most devout Jains wear face masks, go shoeless and sweep the ground in front of them as they walk so as not to breathe in or step on any insects. I'd also heard they didn't keep their food in refrigerators, to avoid killing millions of microbes every time the refrigerator door closed. This concern for bugs was something that many sanitised Westerners found astonishing.

We rolled down the valley, occasionally dodging smoke-belching buses labouring up the incline. After crossing the wide river several times we turned into the splendid gates of the temple compound. Ranakpur is no tourist ruin, but a living temple. A festival had just started, and the complex was even busier than usual. Thousands of people filed in and out of the various temples like rows of determined ants, and we had to edge our bikes carefully through the crowds until we found a small parking space near the main temple.

'Please open shoes here,' instructed the sign outside the doors. Judging by the dozens of pairs of sandals, boots and slippers lined up in neat rows, many visitors had 'opened shoes' there already.

Lily took the shoeless group through the entrance, where they and their bags were inspected for forbidden leather items by two grim-faced guards sporting military uniforms. In spite of our warnings to leave all offending wallets and belts in the support truck, several of the bikers were caught out by this efficient pair. Lily called me over and I filled up a bag with the contraband wallets, cameras and belts.

'I'll just be over there running a market stall,' I joked. 'Should get a few bob for some of these cameras. Are those real Gucci or Bangkok Gucci bags?'

I'd been into the main temple several times before, so I waited outside with Imran and Ratan near the parked bikes and the rose garden. The group seemed to be taking its time to look at each and every one of the 1444 carved marble pillars inside. I could understand it though; the temple struck awe into every visitor. The women in many-coloured saris, the saffron-robed monks and the dangling garlands of marigolds made a striking contrast to the white pillars. It took time to take it all in.

As Imran, Ratan and I loitered in the shade of a wall chatting about their plans on our return to Delhi, crashing and clanging erupted from the garden on the other side of the wall. We stood up and peered over into the enclosed garden. A couple of gardeners raced towards a small band of marauding monkeys, banging on steel pots to scare them away from the prized rose bushes. The monkeys sneered at their attackers and loped off over the wall, grabbing handfuls of sweet rose petals on their way and stuffing them into their mouths.

While the monkey chasers were occupied with this band, another group surreptitiously leapt the wall near us and lunged towards the roses. The rose guardians bellowed at the new intruders and rushed over clanging their pots. As they neared the second bunch, the first group made another advance toward the prize roses. By now the frustrated gardeners were near-hysterical, running every which way and banging the pots. Eventually, the gardeners split up, mounted a concerted offensive, and drove all the monkeys to the other side of the wall. For the time being, an uneasy and probably very temporary truce prevailed between the rose thieves and the gardeners.

'Why don't they use catapults or even just throw stones?' I asked Ratan.

'Oh not possible for Jains. Very holy people, not hurting animals,' he said, then strolled along the wall to just below where the second group of monkeys sat and pulled a handful of peanuts from his pocket. In an instant, the animals were all around him, hands outstretched and demanding a treat. They were assertive but not aggressive, but mindful of rabies or at the very least, a nasty bite, I refused Ratan's offer of some peanuts. Several times in the past I'd noticed him sneaking off for a few moments to feed monkeys.

'Why do you always feed these animals? You'll get bitten if you're not careful.'

'I don't think so,' he smiled. 'Hanuman the monkey god is my special god and he will protect me. If I did get bitten, perhaps I have done something wrong.'

I shrugged, hoping his karmic bank account was well in credit.

Eventually the group re-emerged in dribs and drabs. Karen and Owen, who tried not to miss any photo opportunities, were the last ones out. Karen looked a little sheepish.

'What's up? I asked.

'I got whistled at,' she said.

Photography is allowed inside the temple if you pay forty rupees for a camera permit, but photographing of idols isn't. While taking a photo of some pillars she'd accidentally pointed her camera at a small statuette hidden in the gloom. A guard had rushed up and blown a whistle at her, shouting, 'Hello! No photographies of idols please!' Being stared at by hundreds of Indians can be discomfiting at the best of times, and it's even more embarrassing when the guilty party is caught breaking religious rules.

By this time our stomachs were demanding some lunch. Normally the lunch hall provides an excellent lunch for fourteen rupees per person, but because of the festival, the crowds were being fed for free in another compound. We followed a group of worshippers striding purposefully across the grounds, and found ourselves inside a long, wide, open-sided hall. A line of women ladled rice, dhal, sweet vegetables and puris from huge vats onto metal plates almost the size of dustbin lids. After asking several times if it was all right for us to join in, and being assured that we were most welcome, each of us grabbed a plate and joined the queue.

'Do you think this food is safe to eat?' asked Warren, who wasn't a great fan of Indian food. He looked dubiously at his plate.

'I guess we'll find out', Ken said, helpfully. 'Either it is, and we'll be fine, or it isn't and we'll all be violently ill.'

'Oh' said Warren. 'I might just have a bit of rice.' He looked around. 'Where's the cutlery?'

Alex smiled. 'I think you're holding your plate with it.'

Warren looked puzzled. Alex waggled his hand. 'Fingers' he said, and moved away.

I went off to find a spot to sit and eat my lunch as politely as possible. Over our years in India Lily and I had had quite a bit of practice, and we managed not to drop anything on ourselves. Watching our Western bikies trying to shovel dhal and rice into their mouths with fingers and chapatis was not a pretty sight. Afterwards, there was plenty of dabbing at messy shirt fronts and hand-washing under a nearby tap.

As we were putting our packs back on the Bullets Lily opened her bag and sniffed inside it.

'Yuck', she said, holding out the bag. The hard-boiled egg she'd pinched from the breakfast table in Udaipur had smashed all over her books and jacket.

'Oh no', groaned Karen, looking inside her own bag. 'All over the camera, too.'

'We shouldn't have brought eggs into a vegetarian temple', sighed Lily.

'Or pointed cameras at gods', added Karen, wiping yolk off the lens.

On our way to the temple we'd passed a lone stone hut perched up on a rocky hillside overlooking peaceful green fields. 'Harmony Restaurant' read the sign mysteriously. On our return journey the owner was sitting waiting for us, and as we drove up the road he stood up and waved wildly. We couldn't pretend not to see him, and as our throats were dry anyway, we stopped the bikes and climbed the hill.

'Welcome welcome!' he shouted. 'Please, sirs and ladies, sit, sit!'

We looked around. A single chair stood in the middle of the small, polished cow-dung courtyard.

'You are waiting one moment sirs and ladies!' he pleaded. Over the next 'one moment' he produced an endless supply of ancient plastic chairs from some secret chair-storage place. He also handed out back issues of *India Today*, an English-language news magazine along the lines of *Time* or *Newsweek*. These were avidly grabbed by the literature-starved group.

'And what sirs and ladies is having to drink? Cola? Limca? Chai?'

He'd been able to find enough chairs, but supplying that many drinks all at once turned out to be more difficult. Not everyone got what they asked for, and none of the drinks were very cold – 'refrigerator not working'. I wondered if Mr Harmony – who we later discovered was named Mr Mohan Singh, but who we always thought of as Mr Harmony – was a devout Jain. I noticed more than a few of the group surreptitiously wiping the mouths of the bottles with their handkerchiefs or sleeves. I strolled around to the back of the small building and peeked into the tiny room that doubled as his kitchen and sleeping quarters. There was no fridge, and now that I looked, no electricity, just a line of earthenware jugs covered with damp tea towels to keep the drinks 'cold'.

When the drinks and chai had been served, the 'visitor's book' was presented with a flourish and handed around for our signatures. As we perused the past year's entries we worked out that, assuming only half of his visitors signed the book, Mr Harmony had only received fifty or sixty customers this season. It seemed there would be hardly enough profit in this small amount of commerce to purchase the subscription to *India Today*, let alone feed a family.

'How do you manage with so few customers?' I asked him as I paid for our drinks, which were far cheaper than any we'd bought in Udaipur.

'My needs are simple, sir. I grow some channa and vegetables in the garden down in the valley, and I have only myself to feed as my family is all grown and departed. God provides. You will be coming back please?' he asked, shaking my hand for the fourth time as we walked down the hill.

I pictured him waiting for us to come back on the next tour, and his crestfallen look if we didn't stop but just rode on by. It wasn't a 'harmonious' thought. Now that we'd stopped once at the restaurant, it seemed that we had an obligation to stop on every visit to Ranakpur, to ensure that God did indeed provide for Mr Harmony.

We rode the last part of the day's ride, some 30 kilometres to Kumbhalgarh, in blistering heat. Although there were countless photo opportunities of rural beauty along the way, few were taken as we all hurried to reach a cool shady spot.

'Don't forget to drink plenty of water,' reminded Lily at a short stop to wait for the stragglers. A subdued muttering between a couple of the beer-drinking blokes gave the distinct impression that there was no way they were going to waste a thirst like this on mere water.

Finally, at about three o'clock we rode through the last valley and made our usual noisy arrival at the hotel. The sight of the nearly-new luxurious-looking hotel, complete with swimming pool and wet bar, revived the bedraggled bikies. As the bikes were being parked and luggage unloaded and taken to the rooms the cry went up, 'See you back at the pool for a beer in ten minutes!'

Within half an hour one side of the pool was lined with half-submerged bikers leaning back enjoying cold Kingfisher beers. Every few minutes someone plunged into the water, much to the amusement and bemusement of Imran and Ratan who were sitting nearby enjoying a hot chai. Indians rarely swim, and our two support people never drank alcohol.

At breakfast the next day there were two empty seats. Karen and Ken still hadn't arrived. As the waiter was handing out the usual eggs, Karen walked up alone.

'Where's Ken?'

'Ken's not coming for breakfast,' she said. 'I don't think he'll be able to ride either – he's spectacularly, horribly sick.'

With the memories of my excruciating experience with the coconut in Delhi still vivid in my mind, I was sympathetic.

'Did he eat meat last night?' I asked, although this question was pointless because nearly everyone had eaten meat at the hotel dinner, and no one else had fallen ill.

'No, he didn't. He even passed up the butter chicken, and he *loves* butter chicken. He's convinced the lunch at the temple did him in.'

After the crash, the snogging Sikh and now this bout of illness I was beginning to wonder whether Ken was more adventure-prone than was good for him. Although I didn't really think the temple lunch was the culprit – again, nobody else was ill – I said, 'Maybe there's no such thing as a free lunch.'

Lily, always the sympathetic nurse, said, 'He should have had the butter chicken.'

But the last word went to Imran, just before our departure from the hotel on the road to Pushkar as we were loading the near-comatose Ken and his vomit bag into the Sumo after breakfast. It was a tight squeeze. Karen had decided to nurse her stricken spouse rather than ride pillion with one of the others, so she and Ken were both squashed up beside Ratan, who was doing his best to give them room.

Imran had once again come to the rescue and was going to ride the Canadians' Bullet. He gazed at the pitiful sight of Ken's white face propped up against the Sumo window.

'Too much beer and swimming,' he said.

Chapter Twelve

It was two in the morning. In the courtyard below our rooms the music, chattering and guffawing had kept us awake for hours. These weren't the interesting noises of a wedding or a religious event. This was just a bunch of loutish whacked-out backpackers intent on depriving their fellow travellers of sleep. I was considering getting up to shout at them to be quiet when a bellow erupted into the night.

'SHUT THE **** UP!!!'

Instantly there was a stunned, complete, silence. Ken had mustered up enough energy to stagger a metre from his sickbed, lean over the balcony and howl at the noisemakers. For the rest of the night, the only sound was the chanting of priests and clanging of temple bells from across Pushkar Lake.

Pushkar is a holy city. Because it's an important place of pilgrimage, it seethes with sadhus seeking enlightenment and curious Westerners seeking all sorts of things, holy or not. No meat, eggs or alcohol are allowed, although there are a suspicious number of tourists suddenly drinking bottles of cola everywhere. Drugs are supposedly also prohibited, but the streets are full of glassy-eyed Westerners.

I'd first been to Pushkar twenty years ago on the way back to London from Goa, just one more of the hundreds of Western youths wandering aimlessly along the hippie trail. I'd spent a couple of days purportedly finding my inner self, but in reality just trying out various hallucinogens. Back in Pushkar two decades later, some of these faces on the street looked disturbingly familiar and no more enlightened than they were twenty years ago. Velvet smocks, paisley trousers and flowing pseudo-Indian robes were the garb of choice in the seventies and, obviously, neither fashion nor pursuit of 'inner peace' had changed since that last visit.

Pushkar came as a rude shock to our group who, despite their recent visit to Udaipur, had become very accustomed to being the only Westerners in the small, quiet and mostly untouristed towns we'd visited. The famed Pushkar Camel Fair had just finished, and rubbish lay in thigh-high piles in the streets. The lake, though, was still a peaceful place, and we abandoned the street markets for a twilight walk along the lakefront ghats.

On the way back to the hotel after our tranquil stroll around the lake, we passed the ridiculously misnamed Hotel Om. Far from being a peaceful meditative place, this luridly-lit café loudly enticed the night-crawlers in from the street. 'Come in please, sirs!' shouted the doorman. 'Hashish, e, acid?' None of our group took up the offer. Outside the 'techno-chai shop' clusters of young Westerners sat bug-eyed or droop-lidded, depending on their drug of choice.

During the night the yappy Israeli backpackers at our hotel once again played their wretched technomuzak far into the wee hours. It was late, we were tired, and none of us could be bothered to get out of bed and order them to 'shut the **** up'.

I had a better idea.

At the first light of dawn I knocked quietly on a few doors. It was easy to find some grumpy, sleep-deprived accomplices amongst our group. The only guests at the hotel were our bikers and the late night revellers. Breakfast was being set out in the restaurant, so I suggested to my accomplices that we 'ring the breakfast bell' for the backpackers. Starting up a couple of the bikes we roared full throttle round and round the courtyard, revving our engines right outside their doors. It was like a scene from some sixties 'Hell's Angels Come to Town' movie, only this time it was the oldies riding their bikes around the pool terrorising the bemused teenagers instead of *vice versa*. After a few rounds of this, a couple of them staggered bleary-eyed to their doors. We smiled cheerily and bade them 'good morning'.

Having had our pointless but highly satisfying little revenge, it was time to fortify ourselves with breakfast and leave Pushkar to the druggies and partygoers.

The early morning road to Jaipur gave our clients a taste of what to expect a few days later on the dreaded Delhi highway. On the climb up to the pass through to Ajmer, we gradually overtook crawling convoys of crowded buses as they dragged their huge human loads up the incline. Many of them carried thirty or more people on their roofs, sitting atop the luggage. We wondered if the fare for these 'cheap seats' was discounted.

On the way down the other side the same buses tore past us recklessly, brakes smoking, hurrying to make up for time lost on their slow ascent. By this time, each of the group had developed a healthy cautious attitude toward Indian traffic, and there was little anger or indignation at the insane antics of the bus drivers. Our riders just pulled out of the way and allowed them past to career at death-defying speeds down the hill.

After a brief flirtation with the rush-hour traffic around the edge of Ajmer we came onto the main highway, a wide two-lane artery crowded with rumbling trucks and buses. A sign at the roadside warned, 'It is better to be fifteen minutes late in this world than fifteen minutes early in the next!' Not many of the drivers on this road seemed to take any notice.

Over the next two hours an endless procession of heavy vehicles lumbering along at 50 kilometres per hour tried our patience. Overtaking, though, required careful strategy, good driving skills and nerves of steel. Positioning ourselves in a tight group behind a truck, we would wait for a space in the oncoming traffic and, when one appeared, we zoomed out, horns blaring, crossing our fingers that we'd all make it past before the truck driver woke up and decided to overtake the vehicle in front of him. Every now and then a phalanx of three trucks, all straining to overtake his neighbour in a suicidal line abreast, hurtled towards us, only swerving in at the last hair-raising second.

Eventually we all pulled up into the quiet, leafy courtyard of the Hotel Diggi Palace. The hotel, another converted maharaja's palace, was home to Tutu, the groom in the upcoming royal reception. We congratulated Tutu on his recent wedding and thanked him for his invitation to attend the royal reception the next evening. The hotel had been closed for the event, but he had honoured our booking and invited the whole group to this grand spectacle.

As Lily organised room allocations, Karen came out of hers looking pensive.

'What's up?' I asked.

'Look out here,' she said, waving at the peaceful green courtyard. 'Then look out our window.' The windows of the comfortable, colourful rooms looked outside the hotel compound and down onto shacks built of plastic sheeting and bits of tin leant up against the hotel wall. A few puny chickens scratched in the dust, and several even punier children played amongst the rubbish.

'I'm finding this all pretty hard to come to grips with,' she said. 'But I've got no idea what to do about it.'

I knew exactly what she meant.

⁓

Over the years of travelling in India we'd constantly been assailed by the wide disparity between rich and poor in the cities. Our ability to spend a couple of thousand dollars on an air ticket and thirty to fifty dollars a day on accommodation for a casual visit puts us in the realm of the fabulously wealthy, as far as the street people are concerned. Walking around Jaipur, the capital city of Rajasthan, it is impossible not to think about this yawning gap.

All along the prosperous Mahatma Gandhi Road with its chic jewellery, clothing and antique shops, the pavement is lined from end to end with sleeping bodies who live and die on the street. Driven from the rural areas by famine and drought they make their way into the cities, in hopes of finding something better there. They clutch bags containing their few wretched possessions and, as we pass, hold out their hands beseeching us to drop them a couple of rupees. At least in part, the incredible Indian will to succeed is fuelled by these unrelenting everyday reminders of the price of failure. Always in the background, and often right in our faces demanding money, the street dwellers of Delhi and Jaipur are a grim embodiment of the consequences of a nonexistent social welfare system. No economic safety net awaits those who cannot pay for their rent or food.

As we hurried past, these snapshot images of the lives of these

163

dispossessed people only hinted at the miserableness of their day-to-day existence. We had agonised many a time, as do most Western visitors to India, about whether to give a few rupees to these beggars. The act of giving alms to the poor is deeply entrenched in both Hinduism and Islam, and most Indians who can afford to will give something once a day. To us this often seemed a hopeless gesture, done more to soothe a troubled conscience than as an act of genuine benefit to the poor. Despite this, we often slipped a coin to some bedraggled child.

From the first tour, Lily and I had decided to seek out something more positive to contribute than the random sprinkling of a few coins here and there. First we visited an orphanage in Udaipur. Although it appeared clean and well-run, the staff were under the misapprehension that we, like most of their Western visitors, were interested in adopting a child. The director guided us around the orphanage and showed us the most suitable children, in the manner of a shopkeeper displaying his best wares. Eventually, and inevitably, the subject of money came up. The director assured us that for a 'small fee' he'd be able to help us sidestep much of the bothersome bureaucracy involved in adoption. This experience left us quite discouraged, as we had no wish to transplant an unfortunate child into our foreign culture.

Our answer came out of the blue one afternoon near Ranthambhore Park. We'd taken a few hours' break from our group and gone out for lunch in a small restaurant. As we relaxed over our lunch, a couple of blue-rinsed elderly German women at the next table started chatting to us. The older of the two, Elizabeth, was one of those experts on India that one meets from time to time, and she prattled on amiably about all of the places that we 'just *had* to visit'.

Gently we let her know that we were tour guides and visited these places on a monthly basis on motorbikes. Like most people, she was horrified at the concept of biking here, but warmed to the idea after a while.

'You know, sometimes ve haf to close our eyes in ze car, he drives so fast!' she exclaimed, pointing to their beaming driver, sitting at the next table with Ratan and Imran.

'Closing our eyes isn't an option, but at least we have control over our speed,' I replied.

Once we got off the subject of tourism though, her true passion came out, as she described the relief project that she was involved in up in the Himalayas. She worked voluntarily as a fund-raiser for SOS Children's Villages, an international organisation that provided homes to displaced children in a family environment. Elizabeth explained that these villages and families became the children's homes throughout their entire childhood. Adopting the children out wasn't an option. From the photos of her adopted village in Himachel Pradesh and the literature she showed us, the SOS organisation looked like just the sort of thing we wanted to be part of.

As it turned out, our route roughly followed Elizabeth's over the next week or so, and we had several roadside encounters with her. Often she would emerge, immaculate and regal, from the back seat of her air-conditioned Ambassador amongst a dusty and sweaty group of us.

'Ach, my motorcycle friends. Zis is der wunderbar vay to see zer India yah.'

We arrived in Jaipur to find that she and her companion were also staying at the Hotel Diggi Palace. She greeted the bikers like long-lost friends. Taking us aside, she told us she was going to visit the SOS village in Jaipur, and would we like to come?

It was an opportunity too good to miss. After settling the group and showering away the dust and road grime, we got into her car and pushed our way through the Jaipur traffic. The car crawled through a busy commercial district, surrounded by factories and small businesses, the streets crowded to overflowing with market stalls and homeless families. We stopped at a substantial gate topped by barbed wire in the middle of this chaos, and passed into an oasis of calm and order. The guard at the gate took us through into the pleasant shady garden, asked us to be seated and then hurried away to the office.

Shortly, a sari-clad woman in her thirties emerged. She introduced herself as Mrs Shobha Kaul, the director, and welcomed us all. Elizabeth introduced Lily and me as 'her brave motorcyclist friends' who had come to talk about sponsorship. As we enjoyed the obligatory cup of tea, Mrs Kaul quietly explained that the children in these homes had been abandoned by their parents. Some were born out of wedlock, while others were given up by parents too poor or ill to feed them. Each child taken in by the SOS Children's Village was placed in one of twelve families, each containing about twelve children. Every family was looked after by a 'mother', a single woman who had not married and who stayed with her allocated children for her entire working life. The only men in the village were the accountant, village doctor and a couple of gardeners.

As Mrs Kaul led us around the well-kept gardens dozens of cheerful, healthy, well-dressed children bounded up to us, vigorously shaking our hands and asking our names. Mrs Kaul explained that the children were encouraged to go to school for as long as they showed the aptitude for study. Several of these rescued children had gone on to study at university and were doing very well.

The more Lily and I saw of the children's village, the more convinced we were that this was a worthwhile project to support. Importantly to us, it was run efficiently and expertly by Indian people for Indian people, with seemingly excellent results.

Mrs Kaul led us to one of the neat concrete flats surrounding the garden and introduced us to the Roy family: four cheeky boys, six smiling, gracious girls and their mother, Sita. The youngest child, two-month-old Amit, had just been taken into the family the previous day. He'd been found that morning outside the gates of the village, stuffed inside a plastic bag. He was badly malnourished and obviously very ill, wailing feebly and waving stick-thin, scabby limbs. Lily took a close look at him and whispered to me, 'This is a very sick baby. He'll be lucky to recover.' We feared that next time we came to visit, Amit would not be there.

Rakhi, at seventeen the oldest girl, spoke excellent and confident English.

'We went to the seaside last year, to Calcutta,' she told us.

'What, the whole family?' asked Lily, surprised.

'Yes. All eleven of us. My mother's family are from there so we all went on the train. It took two days and was great fun.'

Hearing this, and seeing the natural warmth towards each other, convinced us that this was truly a family environment where they all belonged.

After promising Rakhi to keep in touch by letter and return soon, we sought out Mrs Kaul in her office again, and agreed to sponsor the Roy family. Our idea was not only to contribute to the family ourselves, but to donate a portion of each client's fee as well. Mrs Kaul graciously accepted our offer.

On the way back to the Hotel Diggi Palace we thanked Elizabeth for her introduction.

'Ach! Don't thank me. Thank the good fate that we met,' she replied. 'I'm sure that zis vos destiny yah?'

∽

Nine months later, we took our group to the village to show them just how their donated portion was being spent. To our great relief, Amit had turned from a nearly-dead baby into a chubby-cheeked, sparkly little toddler. Watching him chuckling away in Rakhi's arms made us even more certain that we'd chosen the right project to support.

'What do you think?' I asked Karen as we strolled around the village, followed by herds of giggling children.

'It's a wonderful project. These few dozen kids are all healthy and well looked-after. But it's a surreal feeling. The minute we walk out that gate, we're right back amongst the hundreds of kids with nothing at all. These kids who've been abandoned by their parents are the lucky ones.'

Late that evening we stepped out into the choking pollution of Jaipur's night air after another outstandingly huge and cheap meal at a small dhaba. Immediately we were caught up in the midst of a gaggle of beggar children clad in rags, most no more than about six years old. 'Rupees' they implored, tugging at our sleeves or pant legs. 'Chapati'.

Some of the bikers, torn between irritation and conscience, furtively dropped rupees into their small hands. I went back inside the restaurant and grabbed a couple of chapatis left over from our meal and handed them to one little waif. Without missing a beat she tucked them in amongst her rags, and continued to plead for 'rupee, one rupee'. This band of urchins followed us along the dark streets for a full fifteen minutes before giving up and going off in search of more generous tourists. We walked back to the hotel through the poisonous haze. A few of the sleeping bodies stirred as we passed, but most lay quiet on the pavement, as if past caring.

The situation definitely became more surreal as the last-minute preparations for the royal reception continued. On the morning of the reception, an army of workmen and caterers descended upon the peaceful hotel gardens and began to transform them into a wonderland. Wall hangings in shades of tangerine with intricately embroidered edges were draped around the perimeter of the courtyard and entrance road. The entire lawn area was covered piece by piece with rich, exotic rugs. A catering marquee the size of two tennis courts had been erected to one side and enormous tables, cooking areas and a stage set up.

We'd spent the morning exploring the Palace of the Winds and Jantar Mantar, the city observatory, but upon our return to the hotel for lunch it became apparent that the best show in town was right outside our own rooms. We set up shop with seats and tables on one of the balconies overlooking the gardens, and watched the transformation unfold.

Oversized teetering rickshaw-loads of chairs, some plush, some rickety, arrived and were set out in curved rows facing the entrance and stage, with the most grand and comfortable in the front row on either side of two throne-like silver and jewel-encrusted armchairs.

We wondered where we bikers would be seated, close to the front or on the hard benches at the rear.

In the entrance to the palace compound a seven-piece band consisting of tablas, cornets and a hurdy-gurdy had taken up position. Every time someone approached, they played a welcoming blast of traditional Rajasthani music. Miles of fairy lights and tinsel stretched above the freshly swept roadway to the hotel, and canvas screens had been erected to hide unsightly pieces of wasteland. Brightly coloured lines of emerald green, vermilion, ochre and white tika powders were laid along the road boundary in intricate patterns.

Meanwhile, at the catering tent, wood and charcoal fires crackled in the portable tandoori ovens, preheating them to the blistering temperature required to bake naan breads. 'Cannibal-sized' cauldrons full of dhal, soup and rice simmered atop other fires. Seemingly the entire stock of a good-sized crockery shop was stacked tower-like on the central table, and trolley-loads of soft drinks and beers cooled in freezer-sized bins of ice. There seemed to be enough food and drink being prepared to feed all of Jaipur.

As dusk fell and preparations reached a fever pitch, the first early guests began to trickle in. We hurried off to our rooms to dress for the evening's festivities.

Half an hour later, when we returned, the garden was filling up with scores of male guests. Of the women there was none to be seen. The hotel manager explained that, as at all public functions, the sexes are normally segregated, and a separate reception was being held for the women in another part of the palace – as Westerners, we were welcome to attend either or both. A few of us followed his directions to the private gardens of the palace, where the complicated and sumptuous preparations for the men's reception had been completely duplicated. Seats were set out in front of a stage where a classical trio was playing sitar and tablas to the entirely female audience. We were all offered seats near the front, but it was clear to the males amongst our small group that men didn't really belong here.

We slunk off back towards the 'men's party', and the unmistakable whine of bagpipes. A twenty-piece police band, resplendent in kilts and feathered hats, was alternating tune for tune with an eight-piece traditional Rajasthani cultural group. In our absence four horsemen in white carrying lances had taken up station by the entrance, saluting the arriving guests. The more important the guest, it seemed, the later the arrival, and the more dazzling the dress sense.

Although we had all carefully dressed in our best 'going out' clothes, our bikers' wardrobes were no match for the array of fashion finery on display. Immaculate Nehru-style jackets paired with whiter than white jodhpurs and riding boots mingled with Western-style suits topped with multicoloured turbans, which trailed their tails almost to the floor. Even guests attired in traditional village longhi suits outclassed our slightly rumpled shirts and casual trousers.

No one seemed to notice or take offence at our poor wardrobes, though, and we were ushered to a middle row of seats with a good view of the continuing parade of entrances. Tutu, his uncle and young brother stood in front of their thrones receiving guests. Often, as they shook hands, an envelope was discreetly, but not too discreetly, slipped to Tutu, who then passed it to an aide waiting attentively behind.

Soon after, the welcomes reached a crescendo. A queue of official cars flashing 'Important Person' red lights on their roofs awaited their turn to disgorge their VIP contents. An Army General with his retinue of lesser ranks was followed by an Admiral, who'd obviously left his ship far behind. Next came a plain-suited man, apparently an important politician, shadowed by two stern policemen armed with menacing sub-machine guns.

When at last the most important of the VIPs had been greeted, dinner was announced and the assembly descended upon the prodigious feast we'd seen cooking away earlier in the evening. It was impossible to sample even a tiny taste of each of the dozens of dishes on offer.

After this feast, Lily and I sat with Tutu for a few minutes. We congratulated him on his nuptials and thanked him for his unforgettable hospitality.

'You must meet this fellow, he's interested in motorbikes also,' he insisted. Taking us over to a group of jodhpur-clad men, he introduced me to Paul Singh, who was naturally related to all the other Singhs we'd come to know in Rajasthan.

It transpired that Tutu and Paul had organised motocross competitions in Jaipur in their younger days and that Paul was a keen biker still, riding a late model BMW in preference to the local Enfields. After a few minutes of biking conversation he asked, 'Do you play much polo?'

Much polo?! As if I'd naturally have a couple of polo ponies stashed away back in New Zealand. For once in my life, I had no snappy comeback.

'Not a great deal,' was the weak answer. 'If you'll excuse me, I think one of my clients is calling me.'

Around midnight the music was still playing as the few remaining guests drifted away, and we were the last to leave. As we walked back to our rooms we noticed the substantial remains of the feast being hauled to the front gate. There, a line of beggars and street dwellers patiently waited for their share of the banquet.

Chapter Thirteen

Once again we set off virtually at first light, to allow time to visit the several attractions on the first part of the road out of Jaipur before reaching the main highway. After yesterday's traffic mayhem the streets were spookily empty, with all the shops shuttered up and few people about. Without the clutter of humanity it was easier to see the obligatory – according to local government by-law – pink colour scheme on all the shops and buildings of the 'Pink City', as Jaipur is known.

We were soon on the road winding up towards the Amber Fort and the Delhi highway. Here and there on the road mounds of fresh pungent dung began to appear like large ant hills. Moments later all traffic stopped. A short distance ahead some large shapes approached, and the cause of the traffic jam became obvious. This time the hold-up was the elephant taxis of the Amber Fort.

About one hundred elephants wind their way with their mahouts up to the Amber Fort daily. Whereas once the elephants hauled all kinds of goods, now the only work available to them is carrying foreign tourists up the steep path to the fortress-palace.

Even at this early hour of the day there were at least a dozen elephants plodding up the path. As they walked the elephants carried their lunch, a bunch of sugar cane or leaves, in their trunks and constantly paused on the wayside to snack on some roadside delicacy. Of course the elephants had to share the road with a great deal of other traffic, including motorcycle tours and buses full of gawping tourists, and they did a superb job of slowing traffic to a near-standstill. We stopped at a small chai-stand with a photogenic view of the fort reflected in the lake, to wait for the traffic to clear. As the elephants ambled past we enticed them to stop for photos with bananas slipped from our breakfast table.

We hadn't allowed time to visit the fort and palace, as usually by this point in the tour most of the group were 'forted out'. After one last photo we took to the road for the short trip to the birthplace of our trusty steeds, the Royal Enfield factory.

The factory and its immaculately tended gardens sprawl over several acres. At the factory's gatehouse we were all directed to write our names in the massive visitor's book before being allowed to continue into the complex. Every minute or so a familiar roar could be heard as a new Enfield was road-tested around the track near the entrance.

'Go along to that door where you will be met,' ordered the watchman. 'Be careful of the bike testing.'

This warning was a bit ridiculous, considering the traffic we'd had to contend with on the roads outside the factory for the past three weeks.

As we strolled along the approach road another new bike hurtled past us, the rider changing through the gears rapidly and then slamming on the brakes with a squeal and a puff of smoke from the rear tyre. They're running that one in nicely, I thought grimly, wondering if the new Bullets we'd purchased for the tour had suffered this sort of pre-sales treatment.

At the factory door we were ushered into the office of Mr Chibbar, the marketing manager of the plant. From the photos and memorabilia cluttering his office he was obviously a keen biker himself, and he explained the new models that his plant was developing with undisguised enthusiasm. The Enfield company, he informed us, was in the process of updating the entire look of the Bullet bikes and he was eager to get our reaction to the changes. We told him that a large part of the attraction of the Bullet for Westerners was the 1950s retro styling and feel of the bikes, which the modernisation plans would effectively eliminate.

'Oh, we won't be dropping the traditional models,' he assured us. 'They are the basis of all our export business. These new motorcycles are for the local market only.'

We followed him into the factory, a large, airy hall well lit by windows running nearly the width of the building. The overall impression was of a well-planned facility with easy flow of work and little clutter.

Mr Chibbar proudly showed off the new multimillion-dollar computerised drilling machines, boasting of their sixty-four tooling changes, and a robotic frame-welding machine imported from Sweden. It was very strange to see cutting-edge technology such as this employed to manufacture a motorbike conceived in the late 1950s and fundamentally unchanged since then.

The factory staff were most hospitable and enthusiastic. Their offer of a test ride on the new model was gladly taken up by several of the more technically oriented riders, who fortunately didn't thrash them quite the way the factory test riders had. These keen bikers would have happily spent the whole day looking around the factory, but we had to hurry along. We had a big ride ahead on the road to Delhi.

Outside the factory, as we prepared to start up and set off on the final 250 kilometres into Delhi, I gave my final, but one of the most important, safety pep talks of the tour.

'This is a fast road, but just don't forget that it's a fast road *in India*. Expect the unexpected at all times. We've come this far without too much in the way of disaster. Don't blow it on the home run.'

The road was an excellent four-lane highway with a steel dividing barrier beautified with stands of bougainvillea. Over the past four years we'd watched this road being developed from a potholed and congested two-lane nightmare that took eight hours to travel to this newly paved, four-hour expressway. This was an astounding feat of industry, brought about largely by the manual labour of men and women performing such back-breaking tasks as hauling rocks and drums of smoking asphalt, and sweeping gravel off the new surface by hand with whisk brooms.

Regardless of the new road, riding through the towns along the route was still just like the India we'd come to expect. There was utter chaos at any crossroads, and goats and cows wandered randomly into our path, or even ambled over to the median strip for a nibble on the bougainvillea. Generally though, these hold-ups were few and we made good progress in the first hours.

Still, if any of the group had doubts about how tricky the traffic on this road was, there were plenty of reminders along the way. Several large trucks had run off the road and had spilled messily, and probably fatally, onto their sides in the ditch. At one particularly frightening accident scene a red motorcycle lay mangled beneath the front end of yet another of the despised trucks. Cow, camel and dog carcasses littered the asphalt. Some of them, judging by the smell and the swollen bodies, had lain on the expressway a long time, and would continue to lie there. Only Hindus of a certain low caste would perform such an 'unclean' task as moving dead bodies, animal or human. As Matt later observed after passing a particularly bloated specimen, 'The only fat dog in India is a dead dog.'

A couple of hours into the trip Lily and I pulled over, spotting some of the faster riders stopped by the side of the road. Several of them looked quite shaken.

'We were doing about ninety and overtaking a couple of trucks and a line of camel carts appeared from nowhere coming towards us the wrong way, in the fast lane!' said Alex. 'A couple of us almost bought it there.'

This evidence that many Indian drivers had little notion of what a divided highway actually meant had obviously rattled the bikers more than usual.

'Time for a bite to eat and a cuppa,' I suggested.

We regrouped at a dhaba a couple of kilometres down the road. There was a palpable nervousness among the riders about the last section of the ride, the final entry into Delhi. On the first day of the tour, on the drive to Bharatpur, they'd all seen the complete turmoil on the way out of Delhi and they weren't relishing the final few kilometres.

'Don't stress too much about this last bit,' I reassured them. 'It's not that bad a road and we'll take it nice and slow. Just keep using your horns and try to stay together.'

It was true. Unlike the road out of Delhi south to Bharatpur, which wound tortuously through a multitude of traffic-choked suburbs, this road approaching from the west hooked up with the main airport road. Although it was busy it was also very straightforward, with few opportunities to actually get lost. Even more importantly we had Ratan and Imran, our trusted back ups, riding interference in the Sumo at the rear to pick up any stragglers.

Watching these two and the conscientious way in which they did their job, I couldn't help but think of our first, and worst, experience employing a tourist driver.

But then, what were we thinking, hiring a driver named Manic Singh?!

∞

Prior to the first tour, we'd arrived in Delhi to nervously await our very first clients and to interview potential drivers. Having never before hired a driver we were determined to find someone reliable and trustworthy, someone who spoke good English and knew the Rajasthani roads.

The first candidate was Ratan. If only we'd known then what we know now, we'd have hired him on the spot. But at the time he seemed uncomfortable with us and nervous about speaking English, so mentally we rejected him and asked for the next interviewee.

Manic, a dapper and handsome Sikh, spoke excellent and confident English. Nothing would be a problem, he assured us, and he had extensive knowledge of the whole of Rajasthan. Though I had faint misgivings about some of his advice on where to go and what to see, his words were just what we wanted to hear. We agreed with his boss on a set rate for his services as a driver, the vehicle hire and road taxes.

These misgivings turned more ominous several days later, after we'd finally got the first group out of Delhi in the Sumo. On the road to Bharatpur we made an unscheduled stop at the border between Uttar Pradesh and Rajasthan.

'Why are we stopping?' I asked Manic.

'You are paying fifteen hundred rupees for tax,' he demanded.

I couldn't believe my ears. 'But the tax was included in the price we settled on!' I argued.

By this stage we had the rapt attention of most of our clients. Not wishing to proceed along this line of conversation in front of this audience, I muttered that I would pay now, but we would sort it out later.

Manic only heard 'I'll pay', and his smirk gave his whole game away. Within a few days it became obvious to all that Manic's every move and word was designed to side-track us toward every vendor, hawker and tout in Rajasthan who'd slip him a cut of the takings.

The eastern gate of the Taj Mahal is notorious for the mobs of hawkers who descend like the Mughal hordes on any groups of tourists. On our reconnaissance tour a month previously we'd discovered a little-used western gateway into the Taj Mahal area where we could park our bikes very close and avoid the eastern gate hawkers altogether.

But Manic had other ideas. Just before the turn-off to the western gate, he sped the Sumo from its spot at the rear to the front of the group, then zoomed off to the eastern gate with our unsuspecting non-riding clients on board. Furious at his blatant plan we rushed along behind him, tooting our horn and trying to force him back along our route, but we were helpless to stop him.

When we finally pulled over at a car park, it was seething with souvenir-peddlers. Packs of them surrounded each of our taken-aback clients, pressing on them a motley array of 'marble' figurines, 'real gem' necklaces and paper-thin t-shirts for only fifty dollars, sir.

Manic rushed around identifying all our clients as 'his', the better to line his seemingly bottomless pockets.

'How far is it to the Taj then?' I demanded, barely containing my anger.

'Only two kilometres', he glibly replied, 'but there is a bus . . .'

This was too much for Lily. She exploded, ordering him in fairly unladylike language to stay at the back of the group and be the bloody support vehicle he was paid to be. Manic withdrew, sulking. I had the feeling we hadn't seen or heard the end of this.

As the tour progressed and his mercenary character was completely exposed, his dreams of hefty commissions faded and he became sulky and obstinate. I kept a wary eye on him for the rest of the tour, and it seemed I was constantly trying to undo or prevent some mischief that he'd concocted.

Our eventual arrival at Lalli's workshop in Karol Bagh, with everyone from that very first tour in one piece after our hard ride to New Delhi, was an exhilarating finale for everyone in the group. We shook hands and offered congratulations all around, then drifted down into the shop for cold drinks and chai.

'Mr Steve, I want my money now!'

I broke off my talk with Lalli. There was a furious Manic standing on the stairs. I walked up the stairs, taking him outside and away from the group's celebrations.

'Let's all get together in the morning and settle the account when your boss is available', I suggested, trying to reason with him. There was still the matter of the 'taxes' to sort out.

'Give me my money! I want my money now!' he shouted. 'If you don't pay me immediately I will take all the luggage to my house and you will get it when you pay!'

He rushed off down the alleyway towards the still-full Sumo with his keys in his hand.

I shouted at the others for help and raced after Manic, catching up just as he slammed the Sumo's door shut. He cranked the window up furiously as I reached for the keys, and yanked my hand away from the ignition. I gripped his arm and pulled it outside the window, wrenching it sharply backwards. Just then one of our clients leaped into the fray. He grabbed Manic in a very authentic throat-lock while Lily jumped through the passenger door and snatched the keys.

'Help me brothers, they are trying to rob me and kill me!' screamed Manic in Hindi.

In moments a great crowd gathered. Fortunately, several of the mechanics from the bike shop arrived, along with the rest of our now very curious clients. The mechanics did their best to explain the true situation to the muttering mob. Eventually the shouting and gesticulating gradually died down, and we were able to hop onto the Sumo to retrieve the luggage.

By the time we'd passed all the bags through the crowd and down into the shop, the group of clients was near-hysterical with what we hoped was laughter. Lily and I silently cursed this piece of luck on our first tour, and apologised fervently for the drama that had just unfolded.

'Hell, Steve,' roared one of them, 'that was the best part of the tour so far! How did you arrange that little show?'

As I slowly calmed down and stopped shaking, we drank our now cold chais and warm cold drinks and began to organise the group's transport to the hotel. We'd just sent off the first truckload of luggage and clients, when who should reappear but Manic – this time with a surly police sergeant in tow. Sidling up to me, the policeman grunted 'Muni, muni!' in his best English.

By this time I'd well and truly had enough. 'Oh. You want money,' I said. 'Well follow me then.' I strode off towards the bike shop where Lalli had just arrived.

'This officer wants money, Lalli,' I said, gesturing towards the policeman. 'Could you fill him in on the situation here?'

Lalli explained, slowly and deliberately in Hindi, that the driver had tried to steal the luggage, and that several of our group were overseas politicians who were personal friends of the New Zealand High Commissioner and who were, as we spoke, down in his office writing their formal complaints against this villain, and would the officer kindly furnish his name, rank and number so that they could include his actions in their complaint?

More yelling and shouting broke out, this time between Manic and his obviously bribed cop. It was clear that the cop could see which way the wind was blowing. After profusely apologising to us, the policeman marched Manic off down the alleyway.

This time though, there was no Manic Singh to contend with, and despite the group's earlier apprehension, there was no great drama manoeuvring through the Delhi traffic. Everyone bunched up nicely and was fiercely assertive, bullying their way through roundabouts and traffic lights and using their horns constantly to announce to the world that a flying wedge of Westerners on motorbikes was coming through. It was hard to keep the grin from my face as I hit the horn to warn off some approaching hazard and, almost in unison, a chorus of other horns sounded behind me.

'How are these guys going to adjust to riding back home?' I wondered aloud to Lily.

As we took the last right turn into Lalli's street, Alex pulled out in front of the oncoming traffic and, with his palm extended in a commanding stop sign, niftily halted the flow so that we could all get across. I couldn't suppress a laugh.

'Try *that* in Napier!' I called out. 'You'd be dog tucker.'

We pulled up outside the bike shop. Amongst the chaos of trying to find parking space for all the bikes, Lily and I went around shaking everyone's hand in congratulations. Our relief at guiding yet another group safely back to Delhi was obvious, but the bikies were all on an adrenaline high from the excitement of completing the trip, and were too busy laughing and chattering to notice.

After a cold drink, we started to ferry the group back to the hotel in the Sumo. Ratan was well aware that not attempting to steal our luggage was a good way to get a tip. Both he and Imran were surreptitiously slipped several sizeable and well-deserved baksheeshes by clients grateful for their help and assistance over the last few weeks. The bikes, now riderless, were once again lined up in the alleyway, and everyone said their farewells to Lalli's team and the bikes. It was an exhilarating but sad moment for everyone.

Back at the hotel, a party developed in one of the larger rooms. The ruckus went on well into the evening as the tired but ebullient group finished off the not insignificant dregs of their bottles of duty-free liquor, and the stories of fighting through hordes of psychopathic Tata trucks reached legendary proportions.

After dealing with a few last-minute details Lily and I joined in, able to almost completely relax for the first time in three weeks. Our work was almost done. We savoured the fact that, over this short time, this eclectic gathering had knitted itself into a tight group who were well at ease with each other. Despite the wide disparity in age and backgrounds these clients had all stuck together and looked out for each other.

Ken stood up and proposed a toast. 'Here's to Steve and Lily. Thanks for making this trip far more than I ever dreamed. I've seen things that I definitely didn't want to see, but I think I needed to see. I guess that when you see what the people of Rajasthan have to deal with in their everyday lives, it puts our small discomforts and irritations into perspective.'

We couldn't deny this, and we humbly accepted their toast. But the good humour, tolerance and compassion shown by this group of bikies had made our job remarkably easy, and this had been by far the most enjoyable tour yet. Brian started suggesting plans to meet for a group reunion back in New Zealand in a few months' time. This too was toasted enthusiastically by all with a few more Kingfisher beers.

The next morning after canvassing opinion we took the bikers off by autorickshaw to the spice bazaars of Old Delhi city, where a riot of colours and smells assaults the senses. The logistics of keeping a large group of gawking and dawdling people together in these narrow and crowded streets soon became impossible. After ensuring that all these 'old India hands' had the address of the hotel and were aware of our flight departure time that evening, we left them to their own devices to explore the seething back alleys of the ancient part of Delhi.

We had other fish to fry.

Now that we had numerous Rajasthan tours under our belts, we'd talked with many of our clients about possibly doing another, different motorcycle tour, a 'coast to coast' trip through southern India. It was a ride that we'd done ourselves a couple of times and we loved the tropical southern states, which were as different from Rajasthan as Greece is from England. A large percentage of past riders were keen on the idea, and it seemed an excellent way of expanding our business.

The only problem with running a tour down south was that we had been unable to find someone in that area who could rent bikes to us, nor did we wish to be disloyal to our good friend Lalli. We wanted to investigate the feasibility and cost of sending ten of Lalli's bikes by truck the 2000 kilometres down to Madras to use them on the proposed tour. Lalli had recommended a transport agent to talk to about the practicalities of this idea, and we'd set aside this time to visit him.

The agent's office was in a warehouse full of stacks of goods being loaded and unloaded into hundreds of the dreaded Tata trucks we'd so successfully avoided throughout Rajasthan. As we explained our requirements, we could feel him gradually losing interest in the task we were outlining to him with such enthusiasm.

'This will be impossible sir', he said, triumphantly. 'It is not allowed to transport motorcycles registered in Delhi without a permit from every state that they pass through. Absolutely impossible.' He went back to the piles of paperwork on his desk.

'Here we go again', I muttered to Lily.

I leaned over, raised my eyebrows and, in a low voice, asked – 'How do you think we could make this possible, my friend?'

Glossary

amul dasdur: a traditional sweet milky drink laced with opium

babu: office worker or clerk

baksheesh: bribe, tip or gratuity

baobab: a tree of African origin with a very thick trunk and large edible fruit

baori: stepwell with landings and galleries

beedie (bidi): small leaf-wrapped cigarette

biriani: mildly spiced rice dish

cantor: open-topped bus

caste: Hindu's hereditary place in life

chai: spiced and sweetened tea

channa: chick peas

chapati: griddle-cooked flat bread; also called *roti*

charpoy: Indian rope bed

charras: marijuana

chillum: type of pipe used to smoke tobacco or other substances

chital: small spotted deer

dhaba: hole-in-the-wall restaurant or snack bar

dhal: thick spiced lentil soup

dhok: hardy drought-resistant tree with small leaves

dhoti: traditional loincloth worn by male Hindus

Ganesh: elephant-headed Hindu god of good fortune

garh: fort

ghat: range of hills; also, steps or landing on a river

Hanuman:	mischievous Hindu monkey warrior-god
haveli:	traditional mansion with interior courtyards
howdah:	seat for carrying people or goods on an elephant's back
karma:	Hindu-Buddhist principle of retributive justice for past deeds
kurta:	long cotton shirt with short or no collar
Lakshmi:	Hindu goddess of wealth
Limca:	a proprietary sweet, carbonated lemon beverage
longhi:	traditional baggy trouser/sarong-like garment
maharaja:	also *maharana*, *maharao*, *maharawal*; great king
maharani:	wife of a princely ruler or a ruler herself
mahout:	elephant master or rider
mandana:	folk paintings in chalk on village dwellings
masjid:	mosque
monsoon:	rainy season from June to October in Rajasthan
Mughal:	also 'Moghul'; Muslim dynasty of Indian emperors (16th to 18th centuries)
mullah:	a Muslim learned in Islamic theology and sacred law
naan:	flat unleavened bread cooked in tandoor
nahin:	Hindi word for 'no'
namaskar:	a traditional Indian blessing or greeting with hands pressed together; also *namaste*
nawab:	Muslim ruling prince or powerful landowner
neem:	tropical evergreen tree related to mahogany known for its medicinal properties
nilgai:	large antelope
niwas:	house, building or palace
nizam:	princely rulers of Hyderabad in the 18th to 20th centuries

Om:	sacred invocation that represents the essence of the divine principle
paan:	betel leaf-wrapped digestive
paneer:	soft cheese
paratha:	unleavened griddle-fried bread made from wheat
puja:	offering or prayer
puri:	deep-fried puffed-up round bread
Raj:	rule or sovereignty
Rajput:	'Sons of Princes'; Hindu warrior caste who ruled in Western India
roti:	griddle-cooked flat bread; also called *chapati*
sabzi:	vegetable dish
sadhu:	holy person, ascetic
sahib:	title applied to any gentleman
sambar:	large deer
Singh:	a surname for Rajputs and Sikhs, meaning 'lion'
sitar:	stringed instrument
Sumo:	Indian-made version of Pajero
tabla:	a northern Indian pair of drums
tandoor:	charcoal-fired oven
Tata:	Indian auto manufacturer producing heavy trucks
thali:	an all-you-can-eat meal served on a large plate or banana leaf
tika:	a coloured mark devout Hindus dab on their foreheads with tika powder
wallah:	'man'; i.e. 'chai-wallah', 'waiter-wallah'